RAJA YOGA

OR

THE PRACTICAL METAPHYSICS OF THE VEDANTA

RAJA YOGA

OR

THE PRACTICAL METAPHYSICS OF THE VEDANTA

BEING

A

TRANSLATION OF THE

VAKYASUDHA OR DRIGDRISHYA VIVEKA OF BHARATITIRTHA

AND THE

APAROKSHANUBHUTI OF SHRI SHANKARACHARYA,

WITH

AN INTRODUCTION, APPENDIX CONTAINING THE SANSKRIT TEXT AND COMMENTARY OFTHE VAKYASUDHA, AND NOTES EXPLANATORY AND CRITICAL

BY

MANILAL NABHUBHAI DVIVEDI, B.A.

Professor of Sanskrit Samaldas College, Bhavnagar.

CHHANDOGYA UPANISHAD

BRIHADARNYAKA UPANISHAD

GYAN

Published by

GYAN

Gyan Publishing House
5, Ansari Road
Daryaganj, New Delhi-110002
Phone: 011-47034999, 9811692060
E-mail: books@gyanbooks.com

Distribution Network
gyanbooks.com
India, USA, Canada, UK, Australia, France

ISBN : 978-81-212-2793-3 (HB)
First Published, 1885

2nd Impression 2021

Printed at: Gyan Press, Delhi.

Raja Yoga
Author: Manilal Nabhubhai Dvivedi

RÁJA YOGA,

OR

THE PRACTICAL METAPHYSICS OF THE VEDÁNTA·

BEING

A

TRANSLATION OF THE

VÁKYASUDHÁ OR DRIGDRISHYAVIVEKA OF BHÁRATITIRTHA,

AND THE

APAROKSHÁNUBHUTI OF SHRI SHANKARÁCHÁRYA,

WITH

AN INTRODUCTION, APPENDIX CONTAINING THE SANSKRIT TEXT AND COMMENTARY OF THE VÁKYASUDHÁ, AND NOTES EXPLANATORY AND CRITICAL.

BY

MANILAL NABHUBHAI DVIVEDI, B.A..
Professor of Sanskrit, Samaldas College, Bhavnagar.

यो वै भूमा तत्सुखं नाल्पे सुखमस्ति भूमैवसुखं भूमात्वेषाविजिज्ञासितव्यः ।

CHHÁNDOGYA UPANISHAD.

यत्रत्वस्य सर्वमात्मैवाभूत्तत्केनकंपश्येत् ।

BRIHADÁRNYAKA UPANISHAD.

PRINTED AT

THE "SUBODHA-PRAKASHA" PRINTING PRESS, BOMBAY.

1885.

SOLD BY

MR. DAMODAR ISHWARDAS, KALKADEVI ROAD, BOMBAY.
PANDIT JYESTARAM MUKUNDAJI, MAMADEVI, BOMBAY.

PREFACE.

This little volume is an attempt to present in one connected form what little I had occasion to collect in the form of stray notes on the philosophy and practice of the Vedánta. The first section of the Introduction is the reprint of a paper I read in the middle of 1884 before the Bombay Branch of the Theosophical Society; and the second section which forms as it were a supplement to the first, is reprinted from an introduction I was asked to prepare early in the beginning of this year for an edition of the Bhagvad Gita by my friend Mr. Tookárám Tátyá of Bombay. I am the more encouraged to reprint these contributions, with the pretty frequent requests made to me, from different parts of this country, by persons interested in the advancement of transcendental studies, for allowing them to reprint and circulate the paper which forms the first section of the present Introduction. An attempt is here made to demonstrate the possibility of a universal science of ontology from the stand-point of modern physical science, and to present subsequently a brief sketch of all that A'ryan philosophy has to say on the subject. The two translations that follow complete the series by demonstrating some of the leading and important positions of the Vedánta and finally by prescribing certain practical rules for the guidance and exhaltation of the beginner.

The translation of the Vákyasudhá based on the Sanskrit text lent to me by Mr. Tookárám appeared in print early in 1884. Subsequently while examining the collection of Sanskrit works belonging to the late Azam Sámaldas Paramánandadás Dewán of Bhávnagar, kindly lent to me by his son Mr. Lallubhái I came across a very valuable Commentary on the Vákyasudhá by Brahmánanda, which I made up my mind to place early before the reading public. To this I have thought it fit to add a translation of the Aparokshánubhuti of Shri Shankaráchárya, originally intended for separate publication. With the intrusion of this little bit of personal history to account for the somewhat irregular form in which these notes appear, I lay them before the indulgent reader with a hope that they will prove useful to him in his study of the deep and ennobling philosophy of the Vedánta.

A word, before concluding, about the authorship of the Vákyasudhá. Mr. Tookaram's manuscript is anonymous. A manuscript collection of Upanishads in the possession of the Bombay Branch of the Asiatic Society contains the text of the Vákyasudhá under the name of the Drigdrishyaviveka, and ascribes its authorship to Shri Shankaráchárya. Pandita Pitambaradás enumerates the Drigdrishyaviveka in his preface to the Panchadasi, among the works of Swámi Shree Vidyáranya, the well-known scholar and philosopher of the fourteenth century. The text of our commentary ascribes the Vákyasudhá, presumably called the Drigdrishyaviveka by way of description, to Shri Bháratitirtha, who as we know from the Panchadasi was the co-worker of Vidyáranya. That the composition cannot be Shankara's will be clearly borne out by a comparison of any of Shankaráeharya's works with this. It belongs either to Vidyáranya or Bháratitirtha and more particularly to the latter if we trust our commentator. Moreover the various points of similarity between the turns of thought and expression in this book and the Panchadasi will seem to point nearly to the same conclusion.

I would in conclusion crave the indulgence of the kind reader for the pretty long lists of errata which, owing to the book's going through the press in my absence, have become almost unavoidable.

M. N. D.

Bombay, 15th Oct. 1885.

LIST OF CORRECTIONS.

PAGE.	LINE.	INCORRECT.	CORRECT.
4	7	Read after, " in the waking State,"	through the various organs of sense,
6	1	Relising	Realising
6	18	Instead of XXVI read,	*Nirvikalpa Samádhi* is easily accomplished (of itself), the mind standing like the jet of a lamp protected from the slightest breeze, in the case of one, who through the ecstacy of the pleasure consequent upon the experience of *self* overlooks both the *Samádhis* described before (24. 25)
7	14	*ha Ankára*	*Ahankára*
8	9	imaginary (since	imaginary, since
14	6	*Atman* the (*subject*	*A'tman* (the *subject*
15	15	fancies the	fancies, the
„	19	the earth	the clay.
30	18	hypocracy	hypocrisy

INTRODUCTION.

I.

We start with the phenomena of our consciousness—consciousness of the physical universe, without for the time involving ourselves in the much vexed question of the latter being in its nature entirely *real* or *ideal*. We start at the beginning with objects as they are presented to our senses and our mind; with, in fact, the objcects of our daily and ordinary experience, and try to analyse them. It is to be seen whether such an analysis could ensure to us a grasp of the real nature of the cosmos, the real character of the universe *per se*. If we for a moment look round this room, we see on a little reflection that the tables and chairs before our eyes are not the same as they were two years or two months or two days nay two hours ago. If we go a little deep into the *nature of the thing*, we pass, in rapid succession over a series of things,—the tree that supplied the plank, the soil that nourished the tree, the sun and rain that fertilised the soil—I say we pass over a series of changes ending at some inexplicable *atom* or absolute factor in the far-reaching regions of space. Arguing again from the analogy of this analysis, we can easily imagine these things as working within themselves the shape of a something, unknown and unperceived, yet inevitable, a something carrying us through all the stages of its future evolution to the insoluble unknown whence these things emanated. The sun again rolls forth every morning in rosy splendour from the depths of Infinity and returns every evening to the abode of his birth. Night follows day; the seasons roll on in their pleasant and uniform order; the heavenly bodies keep regular time to the ethereal music of the spheres. Almost every instant we see the sprouts of childhood blooming into youth, expanding into manhood, degenerating down to old age and fading far away into the realms of the unknowable and the invisible. What is then the essence of this universe, the real nature of the phenomena presented to our consciousness? The universe appears at best to be the formation, the growth, of years of deligent change, the result of the immutable action of causes unknown and unperceived by the limited apparatus of our mental vision. Even while we are mentally passing over these changes, while we are reflecting upon the phenomena of our consciousness what are we pre-eminently conscious of? A series of facts following one upon another—a fixed order, a change in our mental impressions—all limited by *space* in *extension*, and *time* in *intention*. We are conscious then ultimately of time and space implied by the fixed order insperable from our modes of thinking. What are time and space? As represented to our consciousness they are but a series of changes succeeding one another.[*] Thus we are able to perceive that in fact the very laws of our consciousness necessarily compel us to look upon things as constituted of a series of changes. It is this change, this drama of transition, this puppet—show of time that has engaged the attention and exhausted the energies of scientists and philosophers, ancient and modern. It is this change that has in all times been the moving-spring of the human mind. What fond creature charmed with the rosy allurements of sensual gratifications, what proud warrior riding high over the heads of his overbearing foes, would dispise his pleasures and gratifications, would feel as it were surfeited, disgusted, with his life and the food he lives upon, were it not for this change, this mutation, this overpowering terror of the sweeping and unexpected, yet inevitable and irrestible blow of death? Death! yes, it is death, transformation, change that gives us all our philosophy, all our wisdom, all our morality. Who has not reflected in some calm moment over the drama of existence and has not felt lonely, felt uneasy, in the presence of the strange image of Death? Who has not wished to make further acquaintance of this strange visitor? Who has not wished to grasp without fear the inviting, yet cold hand of this awful guard on the gates of

Fternity? What is existence? It is but a struggle against death. What is even *Moksha* (absolution)—a contest with death rather spiritual than physical. With Death we stand upon the threshold of Eternity: Death but brings us face to face with the Infinite, the Invisible and the Absolute. This Infinite we stumble upon at every step, at every thought. Pursue your investigations how far soever, there will ever present to your consciousness a residue, a factor, inexplicable and insoluble: and here we stand face to face with the Eternal, the Infinite, the Unknownable.

It is a trite saying, but one which is pregnant with a world of meaning, that if one could but realise that he has to die, he would die the very instant he realises the fact. Once the idea of the unpermanence of this phenomenal world is on a man, he is not able to shake it off: nay, it presses upon him with so great a violence that ultimately it grows with his life and strengthens with his body. Such a one—one who in fact has got the first of the four preliminary qualifications of a would-be initiate in the mysteries of the *Vedanta* viz. disgust or *Vairágya* as the Venerable Shunkarácharya calls it—such a one I say, would naturally lose all taste for the world and its pursuits. To him life or existence becomes a problem of life-long interest. He wonders at the weaknesses of humanity, at the delusions under which it pursues creations—at best futile—of its own brain. What is happiness?—that grand idea which humanity is pursuing with all its life and soul. Is it wealth? Is it love? Is it power? Is it gratification of the senses? what is it? Wealth but enkindles greater desire with increasing acquisition; the sanctuary of love is pollutted by the demon of separation; power only yields under its own weight; the senses land us in the region of misery and sorrow. None of the objects known to us can satisfy the internal craving for happiness: none supply that joy, that enlightenment which is the essence of all real happiness. Is happiness then to be looked for in a hereafter? Pooh! says the Materialist, the human mind is but the slave of an idea, it yearns for a thing which it is not in its nature to comprehend or acquire. The human mind is accustomed to draw its inspiration from the future, which it is utterly impossible for it to understand. I must, for the present, leave it to the common sense of my hearers to decide whether happiness could be complete or unalloyed by misery, if at every step in life we feel our heart knocking against the ribs, yearning to acquire something more; if above all, we find all that we hold near and dear to our heart overshadowed by the terrible shadow of Death. The mind of every one who thinks must certainly rebel against the idea of holding all his happiness by a precarious tenure subject to the caprices of an unmerciful master. Happiness must certainly be made of better stuff than mere gewgaws—the fragile toys of time. It must by plain logic rest in something, as it were, in a sense, above the Law of Universal change in something permanent and eternal; in that something *which is the very principle and essence of this change*; What then is happiness? Reserving this question for future consideration it is interesting to see how we arrive at the very same inquiry from another stand point also.

Let us for instance examine human conduct. What is human conduct based upon? We are able to determine which of two given acts is better than the other: but we are not, in the present state of our knowledge, able to say of any single act whether it is good or bad, I mean absolutely good or absolutely bad. When any single act is given, every one refers it, though unconsciously, to some standard of the good in the inmost recesses of his Being;—a standard based upon grounds known to, and accepted by the possessor only. This process, which every one of us passes through at every stage in life, requires but to be demonstrated and generalised. The question therefore resolves ultimately into what is good? What is *the Good*? The followers of John Stuart Mill confound expediency or utility with right: whereas Dr. Whewell and others contend that the Right is something distinct from the useful. According to Mr. Mill a particular act is right because it is expedient; according to Dr. Whewell it would be expedient because it is right. Professor Ferrier inclines to the latter opinion when he remarks "In sacrificing happiness to virtue we do not cease to be men, we only cease to be happy men, but in sacrificing virtue to happiness we do cease to be men, because virtue is the preservation and perfecting of our rational nature, and therefore whatever is at variance with virtue is at variance with the preservation of our true being and is *pro-tanto* a curtailment or destruction of our moral and intelligent life."* All conduct must therefore derive its sanction from virtue, from right, from good. But the question still remains what is virtue? What is the Good? The question thus ultimately resolves into one of searching after the *summum bonum*, the greatest good, the highest happiness—happiness in and of the permanent. It is necessary to this end that we must be able to discriminate between that which is eternal and that which is not. Thus we arrive at that preliminary stage through which every candidate for initiation into the higher mysteries of occultism had naturally to pass, viz. Discrimination or *viveka* as the venerable Shankaracharya describes it. *Discrimination* strengthens *disgust*, which sets one thinking. It naturally follows that the neophyte should devote his mind and soul to the study of the Eternal, subordinating all pursuits to the main inquiry and putting full faith in the teachings of science and its interpreters, passing in this manner through the third requisite or qualification of a candidate for occult truth,—requisites collectively desceibed as *Shama and the other five* by the masters of occultism. Having thus lighted upon the right path he ardently desires to unite himself with the Eternal and the permanent, and thus acquires the fourth and last qualification—the desire for absolution (*Mumukshuta*). But all this only by the way. It is important as indicating to those who make light of initiations and occult secrets, of Adepts and their laws, of the true and real signification of the secret doctrine couched in the words of the Buddhist Arhats, the

* Lectures on Greek philosophy.

Vedantic Mahatmas, the Jewish Kabalists or the Mehomedan Suffis. It is useless to hold the light before one whose eye is not powerful enough to bear the splendour of the blaze. It is not every light hand that can wield the double-edged sword of occultism, not every profane sceptic that can advantageously lift the veil of mysticism. It follows from the above that the conditions required to be fulfilled by every candidate for initiation into the methods of the higher inquiry are, instead of being arbitrary or mechanical or selfish, entirely natural in their development and perfectly rational in their strength and consistency.

To turn back then to the subject of our main inquiry. All philosophy as demonstrated above, beings at Death; all science truly such is but a search after the immutable and permanent. This is real Alchemy—the real philosopher's stone—the conversion of the futile principles of this fragile machine into immutable shining gold. Whether this is a dream, a mere creation of the human brain, a something denied to us by the very laws of our relative modes of thought, or a possibility and a fact capable of realisation, we shall attempt to examine in the sequel of these remarks.

We may here pass in brief over the principal results of the inquiries of ancient philosophers, who have bestowed their attention on, and devoted their energies to, the search after the Infinite and the Permanent. I will purposely withhold from this sketch the experiences of Aryan philosophers, and reserve them for future consideration, in order that I may be the better able to show their solidity and universality from the fact that philosophical speculation at all times of the world has always culminated in, and must ever continue to point, towards those very experiences. Leaving out the older Egyptian, Assyrian, and Mexican civilizations which antiquarians assert to be of a class with the Aryan one, I begin at once with the speculations of Grecian philosoppy—trying at the same time to connect as far as I can, the Europe of to-day with the Europe of three thousand years hence. At the outset I would again request you to bear in mind the meaning we have assigned to the word "philosophy." Professor Ferrier defines philosophy to to "The search of the true and the real as they exist for all intelligence;"* *i. e.*, in simple terms the search after *the real* and *the true.* We shall see what each school of philosophy sets up as *the real* and *the true.* To begin then with the Ionic school of Thales. Contemplating the universe from a physical point of view, he lights upon something material and sensible as the permanent principle of the Universe. And *water* or *moisture* he asserted to be this principle. Thales introduced in supersession of the multifarious mythology of the Greeks an element of Reason in the domain of inquiry. He appealed from the senses to the Intellect; and breaking himself away from the mythological disposition of finding the manifold in the manifold, he soared into the regions of rational philosophy which ever aims at finding the one in the many. Anaximander substituted in place of *water*, the Infinite as the element of all things; and attributed to this *infinite* some inherent power of assuming forms. It was reserved for Anaximines to effect a compromise between the philosophy of Thales and Anaximander by asserting *air*—a sort of *determinate infinite*—to be the principle in question. He seems thus to have made a nearer approach to a conception of the mind, soul or spirit. Pythagoras the founder of the Italic school asserted *number* to be the univerral principle—meaning by *number*, law, order, form or harmony. This philosophy was in advance of the Ionic one in as much as it emancipated itself from the thraldom of the senses and rose to the region of pure Reason and thought. *Number* is evidently beyond sense in as much as no sense has *number* for its special apprehension. *Number* is a *necessary form of thought* under which we place or subsume whatever is presented to the mind. Hence *form* which is another name for number, and not matter, is the essence of all things. "Every thing" says Philolaus "should be either limiting or unlimited, or that every thing should be both unlimited and

---

* Lecture on Greek philosophy.

limiting. Since then it appears that things are not made up of the limiting only, nor of the unlimited only, it follows that each thing consists both of the limiting and the unlimited and that the world and all that it contains are in this way formed and adjusted." Next comes the Eleatic school of Xenophanes and Parmenides. The antithesis around which the whole Eleatic philosophy revolves and gravitates is the antithesis of *the one* and *the many*, the *permanent* and the *changeable*. Xenophanes declared that the one was everywhere, it was God Himself. It is in and through God that the universe is a universe i. e. has unity. He did not hold that there was no sensible world; he held that it had no reality, none in itself, but only a reality in and a for the mind of man, which in fact was no reality at all. "He seems to have approximated" remarks Professor Ferrier " to the realisation of a double consciousness, a rational one cognisant of the permanent *one*, and a sensible one cognisant of the changeable *many* having only a negative spurious and relative existence."* Passing over Heraclitus and his philosophy of *change* or *becoming*, we come to the last of the Eleatics *viz*. Empedocle's. He reconciled the antithesis of the one and the many by resolving the universe into four elements fire, air, earth, and water; and evolving the whole universe from them by certain inherent laws of affinity and repulsion. It is necessary to remark at this stage of our inquiry that all the modern notions of European metaphysics from the materialism of Locke and Condillac, and the nihilism of Hume, to the Idealism of Berkley, and the Absolute Identity of Schelling and Hegel, which I am inclined to believe is a pure, rational exposition of Aryan Adwaitism at least in its exoteric aspects, all these notions I say will be found fore-shadowed, though but dimly, in the writing of these and other ancient philosophers. With this remark we may resume the thread of our discourse. The tendency to account for the universe by sensible ultimates being introduced, Leucippus and Democritus the founders of the far-famed Atomic theory ventured forth the supposition that the ultimate elements of the universe are particles exceedingly minute and absolutely small.* The differences between atom and atom were held to be merely quantitative and not qualitative, in opposition to the Eleatics who admitted no difference in the pure Being, and Empedocles who admitted qualitative differences only. The theory of human perception or sensations was greatly modified by this mode of thought. All differences in our sensations of the qualities of matter, arising from the supposed existence of those qualities in the things themselves, were now reduced merely to the quantitative differences in the atoms constituting the things. The world had reality only in so far as quantity was concerned ; as to quality it had no existence beyond the mind of man. The Atomists were followed by Anaxagoras, who insisted on the existence of qualitative differences in things, holding matter in its original nature to be extremely complex. Anaxagoras further asserted from the *a posteriori* argument of design or final causes, the existence of a Designing Intelligence. Professor Ferrier gives to him the credit of being the founder of what is now-a-days termed Natural Theology in opposition to Revelation. Then followed the Sophists, who were teachers and philosophers. They reverted the order of inquiry. Up to this time man was subordinate to nature, but the Sophists looked upon nature as sudordinate to man. Asserting that man was the measure of the universe, that everything in the universe is true only so far as man is concerned and not absolutely true, they would take away from the world the nobler qualities of truth, virtue, morality as only relative, and therefore unreal things.

As many of the theories of Psychology and Ethics current during the present century seem to me to be based in principle on the conclusions of this or a similar school of philosophy it is necessary to devote some attention to the Psychology and Ethics of the Sophists. Man appears to our view as a citizen

---

* Compare the Aryan Schools of the Nyaya and the Vaisheshika with this.

and an individual. The important point to be determined is how much does man possess by nature, and how much is given to him by social relations? or as the Sophists put it, what is man by nature and what is he by convention and fashion? The first part of the question involves the Psychology and the second the Ethics of the Sophists. Whatever nature commands is more binding and authoritative, maintain the Sophists, than what social customs require. This doctrine so plausible in itself opens a door to the inroads of every species of licentiousness. The Sophists however fall into the error of allowing too little to the natural man. They asserted that *sensation* and *sensation* alone belonged to man by nature. To what extent the Sophists admitted thought to be an indigenous property of man, seems somewhat uncertain. They perhaps included it under *sensation*. Professor Ferrier remarks that "Locke afterwards lent countenance to this theory of sensationalism and the French philosophers of the 18th century took it without any qualification." Out of this Psychology would naturally evolve a code of what may be called natural Ethics. To a creature made up of sensations, the law of self-preservation and of self-enjoyment must be the most authoritative of all commands. Such a being must seek his own gratifications and avoid whatever he thinks painful. Whatever his *sensations* bring home to him as true and real is true and real *for him*, whatever it may be *in itself*. Such a code of natural Ethics will find itself in conflict at every step with the code of social Ethics. The Sophists brought out the opposition between social and natural Ethics in clear light, but offered no compromise. Might was with them the ground of moral obligations, and the fear of drawing injustice upon ourselves at some future time was the ground of all justice. Thus all moral obligations derived their strength and sanction from their tendency to promote and maintain the well-being of society—a foreshadowing, remarks Professor Ferrier, of the modern theory of Utilitarianism. The Sophists were followed by Socrates who asserted that *thought* and not *sensation* belonged to man by nature.

The knowledge derived from the senses would at best enlighten one as to the depth of his ignorance, but the light emanating from a rigid contemplanation of *self* would dispel all darkness and delusion. Hence Socrates adopted as the maxim of his philosophy "know thyself." Socrates held with all ancient moralists that the chief end of human existence is happiness, which he defined as that which may be its true welfare and not an illusory or apparent one. The true happiness of man centres in his obedience to the law of his essential being—and not in his obedience to the dictates of unessential being. The law of men's true being he expressed as "Freedom," freedom from the yoke of sensation, passions, desires. Man's true happiness is thus centred according to him, in self-contemplation and in living according to the law of his higher Being. Passing over some unimportant schools of philosophy we come at once to Plato, the great disciple of Socrates, and the founder of the modern Idealistic school of philosophy. "The farfamed *Idealism* of Plato," remarks Mr. David Masson "is in fact a theory of the cognisability of the Absolute. Our phenomenal world, Plato loves to fancy, is not so utterly and hopelessly disconnected from the Absolute world of Noumena, Ideas or Things in themselves, but that for the pure and persevering reason a passage from the one to the other may be possible."* Plato aimed at correcting the inadvertencies incident to ordinary or natural thinking—inadvertencies which were the basis of the philosophy of Sensationalism; and at confuting the sensational creed of the Sophists. Plato argues deductively that the objects of our superficial thought are but the hieroglyphics of *ideas* in the Demiurgic mind, which ideas are the basis of all real knowledge. He means to inculcate that the mind being by its *very nature* in possessions of these *ideas*, it requires only persevering and hard meditation to awaken it to a sense of the existence of this latent treasure in its deeper recesses. But what is an *idea?* Ideas are necessary truths, like the axioms of Geometry, for *all* minds—truths the contray of which is

* Recent British Philosophy.

absurd and inconceivable. Ideas are "principles by which the variety and multifariousness of our sensible impressions is reduced to unity." Plato, moreover, insisted upon these *ideas* being *innate*, thus importing into philosophy the idea of a previous birth and transmigration. He further extended his remarks to the nature of the soul and asserted that justice was its Being or well Being and that justice means a proper balance of the attributes of the soul. Just as a proper balance of the different organs of the body procures health, so justice is nothing else than the health of the soul. Aristotle found fault with the *idealistic* theory of Plato, as being a mere poetical fancy, contradictory in itself, in as much as ideas are represented as the essence of things and yet as existing apart from those things. In his work entitled Metaphysics or first philosophy Aristotle treats of the principles common to all things, the universal constituents of Being. The elements of being are asserted to be four in number. Matter which is explained as a mere potentiality, a something capable of passing into the actual; Form or Essence meaning thereby a correlative reality existing in the objects themselves, and answering to the conception in our mind,—in fact the Platonic Ideas under another name ;—the moving or efficient cause; and the end or final cause. This philosophy terminates in a sublime Theology. " Although *matter* never exists without *form* and although the *forms* or *essence* of *matter* never exist apart from *matter*; there is nevertheless a *form* or *essence* which exists separate from all matter; and this is the first great cause of all. . . . . This cause is the Deity, the Godhead which moves all, but is itself unmoved." In his Ethics, Aritotle considers the question of happiness, or the *summum bonum*. He places it partially in virtue desired for its own sake, but principally in a life of intellectual contemplation. He placed " man's good in a conscious and active and rational life of the soul in accordance with virtue or excellence, and carried on in favourable circumstances." Passing over the more familiar Stoicism of Zeno and the Hedonism of Epicurus—both of which were transferred to Rome after her subjugation of Greece—we come to the Neoplatonic school of Plotinus who flourished about the beginning of the 3rd century of the Crhistian era. His philosophy is generally described as a mixture of Paganism and eastern mysticism but it suffices for my purpose to remark that his teachings were more or less *Adwaitee* in their character, great part of them being picked up by him in his travels through Persia and other Eastern countries.

A period of about more than 1300 years intervenes between the point at which we have arrived, and the beginnings of scientific investigation in modern times under the Royal srciety of London and other similar European institutions. I cannot with out transgressing the limits of my inquiry, even if I had sufficient materials at my command, enter into a detailed statement of the various vicissitudes through which the human mind has passed during this period. It will be quite sufficient for our purpose if I give a broad hazy outline of the various steps leading from the past to the present. In bringing the history of Greek philosophy to a close we have outstripped the limits of historical chronology. At the time when Asiatic Greece had accepted the sovereignty of Persia the condition of Greek philosophy was far from being stable and established. The Persian Empire was at this time very extensive in its territorial possessions and rich in its intellect, and science. Frequent attempts were made by Grecian sovereigns to rescue Asiatic Greece from the yoke of Persia but without success. At length Alexander of Macedonia the disciple of Aristotle, undertook an expedition into Asia. He conquered Egypt, laid the foundation of the city of Alexandria, and conquered great part of the Persian Empire. "A prodigious stimulus" writes Mr. J. W. Draper "was thus given to Greek intellectual activity. There were men who had marched with the Macedonian army from the Dnubc to the Nile, from the Nile to the Ganges. They had seen the Pyramids which had stood for 20 centuries. . . . . In Babylon there still remained its walls once more than sixty miles in compass and after the ravages of three centuries and three conquerors still more than 80 feet in height; there were still the ruins of the temple of cloud-encompassed Bel, on its top was planted the observatory wherein the weird Chaldean astronomers had held nocturnal communion with the stars. . . . . If Chaldea, Assyria, Babylon, presented stupendous and venerable antiquities reaching far back into the night of time, Persia was not without her wonders of a later date. . . . The Persian Empire from the Hellespont to the Indus, was truly the Garden of the world."* The military talent fostered by these marvellous campaigns led to the establishment of "the mathematical and practical schools of Alexandria, the true origin of Science." After the death of Alexander, Ptolemy Soter, his step-brother, who had accompanied him through his campaigns, became Governor of Egypt. The credit of laying the foundation of the great museum of Alexandria—the birthplace of modern science—is due to him. The library of Alexandria contained more than a hundred thousand volumes, and contributed to human knowledge all or perhaps even more than, what modern science has achieved. About this time followed the spread of Christianity over the whole of the Roman Empire, and the celebrated Trinitarian controversy of Arius—an inhabitant of Alexandria—led to the suppression and dispersion of the Alexandrian library, under an *edict* of the emperor Theophilus. The Bible was hereafter set up as the only and correct test of all scientific research. About the beginning of the 7th century ensued the conquest of the Byzantine Empire and part of Africa by the Persians. This event was followed by the great Saracen invasion of Europe—which ended in the conquest, and conversion to Mahomedanism, of Northern Africa, and parts of Southern Europe. Alexandria, Carthage and Jerusalem—the birth-place of Christianity—were taken by the Mahomedans, who did not care to spare the city of Alexandria also. These rapid excursions of Eastern nations, as well as the crusades which followed, brought the West in direct communion with the civilizations and sciences of the East. In about 500 years fol-

* History of the conflict between Religion and Science.

lowed the sack of Constantinople by the Mahomedans, and the Southern Reformation. An impetus was given to science and inquiry which resulted in the Inductive philosophy of Bacon and other philosophers and in the establishment of the modern-brith-place of science—the Royal Society of London. Thus we arrive at the discoveries of modern physical science, at the unparalled splendour of the civilization of the 19th century. Before proceeding to examine the conclusions of modern science, and showing the ultimate haven to which it is unconsciously drifting—the solid and unique, yet the oldest, progenitor of all philosophy and religion viz. Aryan Adwaitism,—I will pause to make a few observations important in their bearing on the subject of our inquiry. The foregoing review of ancient philosophy proves to us :—

(1.) That the search for the truth is as old as the world or at least as the mind of men ; and that therefore the religion which adopts for its maxim "There is no religion higher than truth" is nothing new, but only another form of the eternal contest.

(2). That the great intellectual cataclysms which have followed, one another in rapid succession might have led to the disappearance of a few brilliant stars of genius—the custodians of the higher methods of inquiry—the masters or Mahatmas of today,—men belonging to such orders as those of the Rosicrusians ; or persons of a class with Appolonius of Tyanna and others ;—and that these might have formed from time immemorial the nucleus of an occult brotherhood of teachers and philosophers.

(3.) That modern philosophy guided by modern physical science is breaking upon ground, trod, more than once, by ancient investigators and philosophers.

(4.) That the march of civilization and philosophy has steadily been from the East to the West—a fact corroborated by History, and brought into prominent relief by our taking into consideration the severance of the United States from their mother country, and the point of civilzation and intellectual development to which they have reached. Sufficient argument exists for us to hope for the return of this lost child of science and philosophy to its motherland—India,—an event of the possible realisation of which the modern religious stir may fitly be discribed as the rosy forerunner.

We must, at this stage of inquiry, start with the conclusions of modern science rather than go over the various steps by which they have been arrived at. It must be carefully noted that the old problem of search after the truth is still the same only in another form. The theological argument for the existence of the soul and a spiritual universe has lost its strength against the repeated attacks of Reason and Science. The problem, at the present day is religion shrinking before Physical science ; theformer deriving its support from blind faith, the latter from free thinking; one resting its hopes of happiness on a hereafter, the other searching for the same in this world. This is the great crisis all round the world, a death-struggle in which one or other must virtually give way to its opponent. Religion declares one thing to be the truth, science, another; which is in the right? Religion with its eyes fixed on Heaven or Science with its looks confined to this universe? Are Religion and Science, then, so far opposed to each other as to exclude the one from the domain of the other? or are they but different aspects of viewing the same thing? One of the greatest thinkers of the present century, Herbert Spencer remarks " that religion is divine and science diabolical is a proposition, which though implied in many a clerical declamation, not the most vehement fanatic can bring himself to assert. And whoever does not assert this must admit that under their seeming antagonism lies hidden an entire agreement ',* I have reasons to hope and believe there really ought to be such an agreement between Religion and Science; and that they must be nothing

---

* First Principles.

more nor less than "Twin sisters" as Professor Huxley has chosen to call them. In order therefore to show this relation between religion and science, we must begin our inquiries, however feebly I may be able even to indicate the lines of the gigantic intellectual task, I say we must begin our inquiries from the stand point of modern physical science.

Although in all ages philosohy tries to go a—head of science yet it is a patent fact that the latter always modifies the conclusions and retards the progress of the former. "However earnestly we may contend for such a notion of philosophy as shall keep up the tradition of it as something more than science, yet the perpetual liability of Philosophy to modifications at the hands of science is a fact obvious to all."* The advance of physical science in recent times, has so far affected philosophical research as to divide Philosophy into a number of schools and systems opposed to one another, in their views upon Psychology or science of the mind, Cosmology or the theory of the universe and its generation, and Ontology or the theory of the government of the Universe or Cosmos. The Sensationl school of the mind deriving knowledge from experience, is opposed to the Transcendental school holding the mind to be orginally in possession of certain innate ideas which require to be developed. The Realistic or Materialistic school arguing for the cosmos an existence and reality in itself, stands confronted by the Idealistic school reducing all phenomena to affections of the sentient mind. There are lastly those who believe in the existence of a first cause-a personal Creator; or those again who stand for extreme Nihilism or perfect Agnosticism; all opposed again, to the German exponents of Absolute Identity. I confess my inability without chart or compass, to steer clear of shoals and rocks on the tempestuous ocean of metaphysics; and therefore leave the achievement to higher and better provided experts. Nor should I be understood to attempt the foolish feat of adding even so much as a straw to the august fabric of ancient philosophy. I venture at best, to present to you in a connected

* Recent British Philosophy by David Masson.

form the opinions of the leaders of science and metaphysics—trying to reconcile where possible, the conclusions of modern investigations with the time-honoured truths of Aryan Adwaitism or Theosophy. I shall for this purpose slightly reverse the order of inquiry and begin first with the Cosmology of the Realists or Materialists—in short, of modern physical science. Science starts with the phenomena of the physical Universe which it reduces into Matter and Energy—which again are assumed to be co-existent and co-extensive. Further, science teaches us that matter exists in one or other of three states: solid, liquid or gaseous; and that the material *Elements* into which all complex objects can be resolved are about 65 in number. Lastly there is the Evolution hypothesis which derives the Universe *as it is* from very rare nebulous matter, through a number of well-marked stages of development. I am of opinion that these facts underlie every known scientific theory about the explanation of the Cosmos. Speculations of various character, however, based on experiments in different directions, have, in recent times, poured forth a flood of light on the field of our mquiry. There are three such speculations bearing severally on the form of matter, the states of matter, and the number of Elements; and first then of *The form of matter*. It was Newton, I believe, who revived the Atomic Theory of Democritus and Leucippus. "Boscovich and others endeavoured to dispense with the Atom altogether substituting in its place the conception of a mere geometrical point which is a centre of force, as it is called. . . . . The latest and most recent speculation revivss the Atom, but not "strong in solid singleness" like those contemplated by Leucretius,—much rather yielding to the least external force, and thus escaping from the knife or wriggling round it; so that, it cannot be cut, not however on account of its hardness, but on account of its mobility, which makes it impossible for the knife to get at it. This is the vortex-atom Theory of Sir W. Thomson dimly foreshadowed in the writings of Hobbes, Malebranch and others but only made distinctly conceivable in very recent times by the hydrokinnetic researches of Hemholtz."* Remembering then that the universe began with a series of something like vortices in the universal ether, we pass on to *The states of matter*: The states of matter are ordinarily known to be three. The tendency of modern speculations about the constitution of matter has been to attribute the phenomena of matter to vortices or motions of universal Ether, which therefore must be considered the highest and last state of matter, known to us. Thus we come to the existence of a state beyond the gaseous one, and are able to say that the states in which matter exists are not three, but four. We may halt at this stage and see whether we can find out a fifth state of matter to correspond with the *Tejas* or fiery state of Aryan philosophy. The state in which matter exists while undergoing chemical combination presents properties peculiar to itself *viz.* vibration, heat and, when the rate of combination is rapid, light also. This state may be described by a separate name. We may for the present call it the "fiery state," and place it between the liquid and the gaseous states. The highest state of matter known to us would accordingly be the ultra-gaseous or Ethereal state, competent by its inherent potentialities of evolving from, and sustaining in itself the whole of the physical universe. The possibililty of reducing all physical phenomena to a certain number of chemical Elements may appear to militate against such a hypothesis, but the observations and experiences of eminent physicists point towards the conclusion that all the different Elements are but *structural modifications of one original substance.* It remains therefore to see what becomes of the 65 or 75 *Elements*? This question may best be answered in the words of one of the ablest professors of Physical Science, Professor Alfred Daniell M. A. He says "These kinds of matter are called Elements. They are considered to be distinct kinds of matter, and are called separate Elements simply as a confession of our relative experimental impotence, and of our complete failure up to this time to break up any one of them

* The Unseen Universe by B. Stewart and P. G. Tait.

into simpler substances, or to build any one up by any synthetic process. * * * Now evidence of a speculative character based (Mandeljifl and Newlands) upon the remarkable relations existing between the chemical properties of the Elements and their atomic weights, and of a directly observational character based (Lockyer) upon the results of spectrum analysis as applied to the stellar bodies—which seems to show that many elements are decomposed by intense heat into simpler elements—lends support to a belief which is rapidly gaining ground that all the Elements differ from one another only in their intimate structure and have a common basis which may possibly be hydrogen: or in other words that all Elements are structural modifications of one form of matter. Thus even the Alchemists' dream of the transmutation of metals cannot now be treated with such unmitigated contempt as it received 30 or even 10 years ago, though it may continue to be a dream to the realization of which no approach is possible on account of the necessary limitations of our experimental apparatuses."*

Thus we see that recent investigations in Science tend to prove the existence of but one Element, one material cause, capable in itself of evolving the whole physical universe from it. Energy exists in Ether, potentially, and becomes known only in its active manifestations, in its kinnetic forms.

Let us at this point compare the Adwaitee doctrine of evolution with the conclusions of physical science. We shall not only find a complete harmony between the two, but we shall find that Adwaitee Philosophy is in advance of Physical Science in consequence (as will be seen later on) of possessing better and improved apparatuses of investigation. The Adwaitee philosophy teaches that the Element (*Tatva*) of this universe is but one—not Ether but Para Brahma with its potentialities I may add. From Para Brahma or *Mulaprakriti* (undifferentiated cosmic matter) proceeds Ether (*Akasha*) with its inherent property of assuming forms (*Shabda*=differentiation or

* Principles of Physics.

Ether-waves ?). Waves of Ether produce air or gas (*Vayu*); vibrations of air produce Fiery matter (*Tejas*); vibrations of which again produce liquid matter (*Jala*); which finally settles down into Solids (*Prithivi*).* Leaving out the *Brahmatatva* for discussion under the second or ontological head of our inquiry, we are able to see at a glance that the five Elements or Tatvas of Aryan philosophy represent the same identical states of matter of Physical Science, arrived at after great research and accurate investigation. Having thus seen that the Adwaitee Doctrine is in perfect harmony with the conclusions of Modern Science let us proceed to examine the Ontology of both :—

Reducing all material phenomena to Ether or *Akásha*, Adwaitee philosophy teaches that this also is an emanation from *Mulaprakriti*, the real and permanent Element of the Universe past, present and future. The Materialistic school of Europe is here divided into two sects: absolute Agnosticism and partial—Agnosticism. The first "declines even the question whether there is an Absolute or not, declaring that question to be equally insoluble by the human intellect, equally irrelevent in philosophy, as any further question about the nature of the Absolute that might follow an assumed affirmative."† There are others like Herbert Spencer on the other hand, partial Agnostics, as I call them, who assert the *existence* of the Unknowable, using the term as almost synonymous with the Absolute, but implying that no knowledge about the *nature* of this Absolute is possible. The partial Agnosticism of Herbert Spencer forms as it were a link between the Agnosticism of the Materialists and the Absolute Indentity of Hegel. Herbert Spencer argues that man can think but in relations, and that thus his faculties incapacitate him for a thorough grasp of the Absolute. The Physical Universe he reduces to matter, time, and space; and shews very conclusively that in mentally thinking of any one of these we are obliged to

---

* Vide Chapter II. of the *Panchadasi*.

† Recent British Philosohhy; David Masson.

fix some limit beyond which we are unable to travel; and that if it were not for some such *limit* it would have become impossible, for us to grasp the phenomena of the Physical Universe. Thus he argues that the phenomenon of our consciousness, though it renders us alive to the existence of a "something beyond" all matter and time and space leaves us in utter ignorance as to the *nature* of this Absolute, which he appropriately describes as the Unknowable. He connects the Universe with the Unknowable and appears to establish between the two a relation of effect and cause. He says that this Universe is but "a mode of the manifestation of the Unknowable," implying the manifestation of the Unknowable cause as the known or knowable effect. Writing about the existence of the Unknowable he remarks "though philosophy condemns successively each attempted conception of the Absolute, though it proves to us that the Absolute is not this, nor that, nor that; though in obedience to it we negative one after another each idea as it arises, yet as we connot expel the entire contents of our consciousness, there ever remains behind an Element which passes into new shapes. The continual negation of each particular form and limit simply results in the more or less complete abstraction of all form and limit, and so ends in an indefinite consciousness of the unformed and the unlimited." And further on "as we can in successive mental acts get rid of all particular conditions and replace them by others, but we cannot get rid of that undifferentiated substance of consciousness, which is conditioned a-new in every thought there ever remains with us a sense of that which exists persistently and independently of all conditions. . . . . . And since the only possible measure of relative validity among our beliefs is the degree of their persistence in opposition to the efforts made to change them, it follows that this which persists at all times, under all circumstances and cannot cease until consciousness ceases, has the highest validity of any."* This certainly is an advance upon pure Materialism or Atheism.

* First Principles.

Let us at this point turn to Adwaitee philosophy and see how far its conclusions tally with the conclusions of modern philosophers. The *Brahmatatva* is described as unapproachable by the *mind* or *speech* of men; and is asserted to be the source and supporter of everything. All things are *of* him and *in* him. Man is not cognisant of this *Brahma* and does not recognise it in his ownself because he views it through *Avidya* or (mental) *ignorance* which accompanies Brahma. Is this not a concise and logical statement of the existence of the permanent Unknowable of H. Spencer? But there is a vital difference between the two. The Unknowable is more negative in its character than Brahma, and Mr. David Masson, I think justly, remarks of H. Spencer that "His Metaphysic seems to me too merely negative."* The Unknowable has no life, no soul in it; whereas the Brahma of Aryan philosophy, is all life, all *spirit.* European speculation has no doubt arrived at glimpses of the Truth taught by Aryan occultism, but it has failed to grasp the spirit of the latter. The ideas about Brahma and Avidya are all there, but the Unknowable, the Brahma of European science, is but a mass without life, a body without soul. We know that the Unknowable *is-exists*; and no science can gainsay this. Further we know that *existence* in the real sense of the word cannot be predicated of anything known to us but of the Unknowable and Unknowable alone. This interpreted in the language of the Vedanta means that Brahma is possessed of the inherent property—existence (*Sat*), or more correctly still that *Sat* is the eternal *potentiality* of *Mulaprakriti.* I am sorry I cannot make my meaning plainer for want of better phraseology, but I hope you have understood me. So far so good. Our *Sat* however means more than a predicative of mere existence; it implies spiritual existence, a spirituality entirely wanting in the Unknowable of European philosophy. There are one or two points which I will lay before you simply by way of suggestion, and not of demonstrated proof, which, in

---

* Recent British philosophy P. 167.

my opinion, appear to argue a spirituality for the Unknowable. To say that there is an Unknowable cause of the knowable effects, and to ignore the *potentialities* of this Unknowable is a logical contradiction. We argue for the Unknowable a spiritual existence, at least an existence in which spirit and matter must be blended into one. Take for instance the *protoplasm* of the evolutionists, the first manifestation or form of *life* as such. How do the scientists account for this *first life*, this first germ of life? They will say that it is a manifestation of potential into kinnetic energy, through the instrumentality of matter. Such a statement will necessarily compel them to accept a something other than matter for the production of life,—a something, the *nature* of which they have not been able to comprehend. Matter *itself* is not capable of producing life. Tait and Stewart express in their Unseen Universe, the same opinion in these words "That *dead matter* cannot produce a living organism is the universal experience of the most eminent physiologists." And certainly the very inability of modern science to show direct, and therefore, according to their own invariable rule of inquiry, acceptable proof of life evolving from dead matter, is a conclusive evidence of the inability of physical science to account for the phenomena of life. The alternative of assuming a something inherent in matter which manifested at some fixed time in the course of nature, will commit the scientists to what we have hitherto been calling the spirituality of the Unknowable. If there were no life in the cause, there is no chance of its appearing in the effect. If the Unknowable had no life in it, it becomes difficult to understand what extraneous element, independent of the Unknowable, can come at some future stage to confer life upon one of its manifestations! Leaving the *protoplasm*, we may examine some of the higher manifestations of life, say man for instance. If the soul of man were but the resultant of certain material forces, how do we account for this resultant being present at places where the component materials are not, and vice versa i. e., how can we explain mesmeric clairvoyance, *Samádhi*, and the so-called spirit-manifestations? The one and only way of explaining these facts away is to cry them down as impossibilities with an air of selfsufficient knowledge and precision, to attribute them to hallucinations of the brain, to ascribe them to imposture and collusion or to thrust them through some unknown trap-door in a corner of the multifarious Unknowable. Mesmerism and Clairvoyance and Spiritualism are nothing new to us. The whole of our system of religion abounds in ceremonies based on the potentialities and capabilities of all-prevading magnetic ether; every hearth in our country has its favourite spirit; every home its good or evil genius. But to the Materialists of Europe the thing means a revolution, an upsetting of all their reckonings, and a confusion of all their beautiful theories and dogmas. It is therefore, one would naturally be inclined to think, that they are so dogmatic, so inimical. It is not my purpose to go into the rationale of the phenomena, but I will quote for your information the opinions of the leaders of modern physical science both for and against the subject: from a review of which you will be able to judge for yourself with what fairness or unprejudice the subject has been investigated. Opinions against and for (Spiritualism.)

1. "Sit with you! no! I have resolved to sit with no one. I made up my mind before coming here that nothing would come of it"—Agassiz (member of Investigation Committee, Harvard University) to Mr. Redman.

2. "They who say they see these things are not competent witnesses of facts."

"It would be a condescension on my part to pay any more attention to them."—Faraday.

3. "Spirit is the last thing I will give in to"—Brewster.

4. "I have settled the question in my own mind on *a priori* grounds."—Herbert Spencer.

1. "Spiritualism amongst its most devout followers is a religion.'—Crookes.

2. "It demonstrates mind without brain, and intelligence disconnected from a material body. . . . It furnishes that *proof* of a future life which so many crave, and for want of which so many live and die in anxious doubt, so many in positive disbelief."—A. R. Wallace.

3. "The spiritualists beyond a doubt, are in the track that has led to all advancement in Physical science. Their opponents are the representatives of those who have striven against progress."—De

5. "Supposing the phenomena to be genuine, they do not interest me."—Huxley.

6. "There are people amongst us who, it is alleged, can produce effects before which the discoveries of Newton pale. There are men of science who would sell all that they have, and give the proceeds to the poor for a glimpse of Phenomena which are mere trifles to the spiritualist."

"The world will have religion of some kind, even though it should fly for it to the intellectual whoredom of spiritualism."—Professor Tyndall.

7. "A most mischievous delusion, comparable to the witchcraft delusion of the seventeenth century."—W. B. Carpenter.*

Morgan.

4. Asked "What is the use of it."? Franklin replied "what is the use of a new born baby"?

5. "The testimony has been so abundant and consentaneous, that either the facts must be admitted to be such as are reported, or the possibility of certifying facts by human testimony must be given up."—Professor Challis.

6. "Already spiritualism, conducted as it usually is, has had a prodigious effect throughout America, and partly in the old world also, in redeeming multitudes from hardened atheism, and materialism, proving to them, by the positive demonstration which their cast of mind requires, that there is another world—that there is a nonmaterial form of humanity—and that many miraculous things which they had hitherto scoffed at are true."—Robert Chambers.

7. "Even in the most cloudless skies of scepticism I see a raincloud, if it be no bigger than a man's hand; it is modern Spiritualism."—Lord Brougham.*

Assuming therefore the truth of these transcendental phenomena we at once perceive that there is more of spirit in man than in the *protoplasm*. In man spirit stands face to face with matter, in the lower types it is subordinate to matter.

There is yet another argument leading to the spirituality of the Unknowable, an argument based upon the analogy of a retrograde evolution, or absorption if I may be allowed to use the term. Solids *(Prithivi)* are absorbed into liquids *(Jala)*; liquids into fiery matter *(Tejas)*; fiery matter merges into Gas

* Spirit Identity : M. A. Oxon.

(Váyu); and gas into Ether *(Akásha)*. It is observable on the face of this series that the lowest in the link has the highest material grossness and the highest the least. The tendency in each stage is towards rarity or fineness, and it may be, in the Unknowable, towards spirituality—towards a something apart from pure matter, yet inconceivable, a something which may be the very essence of both matter and spirit.

Thus we arrive at the conclusion that the Unknowable must have certain potentialities in it, more spiritual than material. Matter and Energy are assumed to be co-existent and co-extensive but their real nature is not yet comprehended. The nature of matter and Energy, as well as of the relation between the two, is still a problem in physical science. "To us the question what is Matter . . . . is absolutely insoluble, ... and as physicists we are forced to say that while somewhat has been learned as to the properties of Matter, its essential nature is quite unknown to us. As little able are we to give any full and satisfactory answer to the question, what is Energy?"* In the Unknowable Brahma, says the Adwaitee, matter is spirit and spirit is matter. The two are in fact different manifestations of *Mulaprakriti*. They exist potentially and therefore the *duad* is but *unity*, which when manifesting itself becomes a trinity. For it is only when the *Logos* (the Son) is born that the Father and Mother (the two manifestations of the eternal substance) can be taken cognisance of. So long as there is no differentiation in the Universal consciousness (*Brahma*)—the universal fifth principle—there can be no individual consciousness to take cognisance of these potentialities.

Glimpses of these truths warranted by modern physical science, and taught by the Adwaitee philosophy of hoary antiquity, occasionally burst through the Materialistic gloom that envelopes the mind of civilized Europe. An eminent writer thus describes the tendency of Professor Ferrier's philosophy. "The inseparability of subject and object, the identity

* Principles of Physics. A. Daniell.

of knowing and Being—this was the doctrine to be hung up in the centre for ever, as the all-irradiating, allglorifying lamp of light.. How it would strike to quick transparance all the gloom! How seen at its highest, as the assertion of one Absolute Mind in synthesis with all things, it need not fear because it could over—match and spiritualise, through and through, and round and round, any expansion of the cosmological conception that science might empirically compel, if even into a vast periodicity from Nebula to Nebula again—clearing as it would the whole periodicity of its materialistic horror or its dread of being shored by a Nothingness; uniting time, past, present, and future in one consciousness; making the stars, once more, but orbs or twinklings of Deity; and filling all within them, to the earth and the heart of man, with his presence and His love!—so" says the writer* "as I fancy did the author represent to himself the consequences of his doctrine." This however is another form of the doctrine of Absolute Identity announced in Germany by Hegel—"The terrible Hegel, the last of the world's great metaphysicians."

Thus we arrive at our main conclusion that the one all prevading principle of this Universe in *Mulaprakriti*; in other words the Universe is Brahma itself. This is a conclusion warranted alike by science and philosophy. This is the truth, loudly and logically declared by Aryan Adwaitee philosophy, the truth round which the human mind centres and gravitates throughout the history of the world.

It is needless to allude to the theory of an extra-cosmic Deity called God, creating and governing the Universe, and dealing out the fruits of our actions. The Universe considered as a whole is unchangeable, but to split it into parts one of which is subordinate to the other, is a creation merely imaginary and fictitious. In a personal God holding himself aloof from his creation, humanity worships but a gigantic shadow of its own image. The Universe is capable of being generalised into

* David Masson. Recent British Philosophy.

Being, or roughly speaking, into a combination of Being and Nothing; but it is very narrow and one-sided philosophy on the one hand that could annalyse it into itself and an extraneous Creator, and blind Materialism on the other that could resolve it into mere void.

When we see that the universe is but a manifestaticn of eternal Brahma, we can easily perceive that our real happiness must rest in a thorough grasp and proper understanding of this universal Truth. Everything besides Brahma being futile and evanescent, must be excluded from that which constitutes real happiness. Our happiness therefore rests in Brahma; in the knowledge of this Brahma, and the joy arising from such knowledge.

At this stagee it is argued that, we are not certain of the knowledge we possess in consequence of the relative character of the instrument of inquiry *viz.* the mind. Adwaitee philosophy supplies a thorough and satisfactory solution of this question and declares its doctrines to be absolutely true and correct —a fact corroborated by the experience of antiquity. I will therefore discuss only this question and nothing more under the general heading of *Psychology.* We receive all our knowledge through the mind. The mind is therefore the instrument of all knowledge. Aryan philosophy however teaches that the mind is not the instrument of right knowledge; and shows that the spirit (*Atma*), or 6th principle of man is this instrument. The mind (*Manas*) is material in so far as it cannot exist independently of matter, but is subordinate to spirit. Mind is but an inferior part of *Antaskarana* the internal organ of knowledge. The Antaskarana is divided into four parts. Mind (*Manas*) which barely receives impressions; Reason (*Buddhi*) which determines upon any particular act; Personality (*Ahunkara*) which underlies all our thoughts and actions in the form of the subjective *ego*; and Selfishness (*Chittu*) which makes us feel an interest in the object under consideration. These with fifteen other organs form what is called the *lingadeha, Jiva* or *soul.* This soul is governed by its inherent

Personality and so long as it is so governed it feels happy or miserable. As long as its Personality clings to a soul it passes through various births and rebirths. It is this personality and selfishness that keep us away from true knowledge. These form what may roughly be described a kind of imaginary *accident* of the Eternal spirit, and cover, for the time this illusion lasts, all true and real knowledge. To illustrate their position the Adwaitees examine the three states of *sleep*, *dream* and *waking*. We feel our interest in things when we are awake, it is half-lost in dreams, and it is totaly absent in sleep. This state of things is explained by the different degrees of *Ahankara* or Personality in the three states. In the waking condition the Antaskarana including the Personality is full awake, and hence the interest we feel in objects, and the actions we attribute to the ego. In dream the Antaskarana is there, but the Personality is only half-awake and hence the unreal enactment of an internal drama of abnormal sights and secrets. In states of dream-less sleep, the Ahankara is *en rapport* with the universal Ahankara (i. e. Brahma). We remember the fact of our being asleep because when the Ahankara returns, memory binds it to its previous mental states. It is in this knowledge of Brahma, that all happiness, all joy is centred. So long as the mind (*Antaskarana*) clings to the spirit, right spiritual knowledge is not possible. True knowledge is of spirit and in spirit; and this cannot be acquired through the mind but by placing one's self, as it were, *enrapport* with the Universal all-pervading Brahma. Real Universe, the Universe of spirit does not stand in the way of true knowledge, but it is the universe of the mind that hinders all progress. For in dreams etc. though the external objects reviewed are not really there, the man feels happy or miserable on account of a purely mental creation; and though these external objects are all the same in sleep, swoon, or trance still the mind being absent, they cause no pleasure or pain. It is therefore, say the Adwaitee, the universe of the mind that keeps the soul away from right knowledge. European science has very little to say on the phenomena of the mind. "When from the phenomena of life" remarks* Professor Stokes "we pass to those of mind, we enter a region still more profoundly mysterious. We can readily imagine that we may here be dealing with phenomena altogether transcending those of mere life in some such way as those of life transcend, as I have endeavoured to infer, those of chemistry and molecular attractions, or as the laws of chemical affinity in their turn transcend those of mere mechanics. Science can be expected to do but little to aid us here since the instrument of research is itself the object of investigation. It can enlighten us as to the depths of our ignorance, and lead us to look to a higher aid for that which most nearly concerns our well-being."

We have ample reason, therefore, to conclude that though Western science and philosophy are not certain of the truth of their conclusions, Eastern philosophy is. And the reason is not far to seek. The former has derived all its knowledge through an instrument of relative validity, whereas the latter has imbibed its conclusions *a priori* or intuitionally from that instrument which is permanent and absolute. I have tried in these scanty remarks to show that the conclusions of modern science also are mainly in accordance with, and lead logically to, the teachings and precepts of Eastern Adwaiteesm. Those who doubt the truths of our philosophy, must raise themselves to that stage of psychical development whence they could correctly test their validity; or if they cannot free themselves from the trammels of relativity and materiality, they must of necessity accept our conclusions on the evidence and testimony of rational interpreters and teachers.

Eastern occultism then declares that the principle of this phenomenal world is *Brahma*, and that happiness, true and real lies in the knowledge and experience of that supreme *Brahma*. The attainment of the highest happiness centres in living in supreme *Brahma*, in carrying out the law of our

* In his presidential address to the British Association at Exeter.

spiritual and permanent existence. It is the phenomenal, the creation of the human mind, that changes and disappears, but there is behind it the *nouminal* which ever passes into the phenomenal and vanishes into its original source. If man but suppress his *personality* and *selfishness*, if he in fact *know himself*, he will stand beyond all pain, all misery, all change. He will live of the world and yet above it. He will be of matter and yet beyond it. He will be with the change and yet without it. He will be one with the Cosmos with supreme Brahma. The nourishing of disinterested universal love for humanity, the suppression of personality, the cause of all human sorrow—are ends within themselves worth striving after and not to be looked down upon with ridicule or scorn. In the mind and its abnormal indulgence begins all our misery; in its annihilation and proper spiritual guidance commences true knowledge, which leads to eternal universal bliss.

II.

THIS fleeting universe has been a school of speculation to thinking minds from time immemorial; and every philosopher has tried to analyse and understand the phenomena about him in the best manner possible under the circumstances. The centre about which the human mind appears to gravitate, in the dark depths of antiquity or eternity, is the change, the never-failing continuous transition, through which every namable object naturally passes. All real philosophy begins, as has been remarked by several philosophers ancient and modern, with Death, we might say, *disappearance* or *change*. The universe, as Sir W. Hamilton puts it, is but a mean between two extremes, both of which, he adds, are inconceivable.* The Aryans call it Máyá, meaning that of which we are conscious just in the present moment, but of which

* Lectures on Metaphysics Vol. I.

we are also conscious that it was not the same in the past, nor is it to be the same in future.* The Buddhists look upon this universe as made up of *Kshanas*† or moments, implying that it is essentially momentary in its nature. We can thus see at a glance that there is a concensus of philosophic opinion on the side of those who look upon this universe as transitional in character, and therefore as something not worth relying upon. We shall try to see how prolific this one universally accepted doctrine has been in India, and how all the principal schools of Aryan philosophy differ from one another simply in their attitude towards this one eternal truth. Assuming that the universe as such is not permanent, the first question that naturally suggests itself for solution is whether it is the substance of the universe that has no permanence or the form of it. Indian philosophy is divided into two great sections on this question. All orthodox Aryans believe that the universe came out from something‡ (*sat*, =*ens*), whereas there are a few, and among them a sect§ of the Buddhists in particular, who hold that the universe came out of nothing. Accepting therefore the logical doctrine of *Everything* from *Something*, we come to consider the relation in which this impermanent Universe stands to the permanent *something*. Before, however, entering upon a discussion of this question, we must decide upon the nature of that something whose relation we want to define. But as it will be both more convenient and intelligible, we may examine these two questions together. There are three theories advanced by Indian philosophers about the evolution of the Universe. First among them stands the theory of creation,|| then comes the theory of $ Conversion, and then the theory of Illusion.¶ The Naiyayikas and the Vaisheshikas, the Sánkhyas including the Pâtanjalas, as well as the Mimánsakas, generally endorse the theory of Creation. The Naiyayikas as

* Bhagvad Geeta Chap. II. 28. † Sarvadarshana Sangraha.

‡ सदेवसौम्येदमग्रआसीत् Chhándogya, also Bhagvad Geeta Ch. VIII. 18.

§ The Mádhyamikas. || आरंभवाद. $ परिणामवाद ¶ विवर्तवाद.

well as the Vaisheshikas, arguing from the effects to their cause infer the existence of a Deity in obedience to whose wish the primordial, infinitesimal, and invisible, elementary atoms of the universe form themselves into visible combinations. There are *seven* or *sixteen* primary elements, secondary combinations of which lead to the variegated phenomena of the world. This is the theory of Creation *par excellence.* Kapila denied to God any active part in the creation of the universe and left everything to the workings of blind nature which he calls *Mulaprakriti* or undifferentiated cosmic matter. From *Mulaprakriti* evolve either primarily or secondarily twenty-three other *substances,* which together with *prakriti* are competent to evolve the universe from themselves. While thus putting the universe upon a purely material basis, Kapila has not been blind to the intelligence running through nature like a conspicuous thread of gold. He gives to this intelligent principle the name of *Purush* and declares that *Purush* and *Prakriti* can never exist independently of one another.* Neither is able to affect or modify the other. Each works by itself, but never independently. The helpless *Purush* guides, so to say, the blind *Prakriti.*† *Patanjali,* while adopting the cosmogony of the Sànkhyas, believed in the existence of an extra-cosmic Deity full of Holiness and Mercy. The Mimánsakas also appear to endorse the idea of an extra-cosmic Creator, who is to be satisfied by Vedic sacrifices and spiritual rites. Thus disposing of five of the principal schools of Indian philosophy as more or less accepting the theory of creation, we come to the Vedánta or Uttara Mimánsa for an elucidation of the two remaining theories. The Vedàntins, resolving the universe into its component parts arrived at Ether (*Akásha*) as the ultimate material link between the known and the unknown.‡ Not only do they apprehend that in every explanation of a material fact there always remains a factor which baffles all ingenuity, but they believe that even of the universe *per*

* Bhagvad Geeta Ch. XIII. 19. † पङ्ग्वन्धन्याय.

‡ Bhagvad Geeta. Ch. VII. 4.7. also Panchadasi Ch. II.

se they know nothing besides the consciousness of certain changes in their sentient Being.* Hence, while believing that the universe commences in† ignorance, they were able to predicate the attribute *sat* (absolute existence) of the unknowable cause, from the essentially indestructible nature of the known effects. Having accomplished this much in one line of inquiry, they applied themselves to a study of the phenomena of their own consciousness, beyond the mere forms of which they were able to recognise nothing in the objective universe *per se*. The mind, they fixed upon as an accident of that something which lies under all the phenomena of the subjective and objective worlds, and determined that that something is the same throughout the universe, unique, equable, and one with the unknown or unknowable *sat*, and therefore Infinite.‡ This something, call it Brahma or anything, being the only one enlightening all phenomena § must be all consciousness|| (*chit*) and bliss. We may state by the way that, inasmuch as through this something we derive knowledge, and knowledge is *pleasure* (*ánanda*), this all-intelligence is all-pleasure as well. The universe than reduces itself according to this analysis into five parts *sat, chit, ananda*; *náma* (name); *rupa* (form). Every namable thing consists of these five attributes and nothing more. The first three are uniform and one in all, the last two differ with each.$ The universe as such then consists of mere name and form, which are impermanent and the substance or *noumenon* consists of *sat, chit* and *ananda* or *Brahma*, which never alters. It is the mind which produces these differences of name and form and causes pleasure and pain by attachment to or separation from them. The essence of this teaching comes then to this, that the universe is but one with, and a part of, Brahma.¶ Here

* Panchadasi Ch. VI. † Idem, Ch. VI. अज्ञान, अविद्या, माया.

‡ Bhagvad Geeta, Ch. VII. 7. 24. also Ch. IX. 11.

§ Bhagvad Geeta, Ch. XIII. 16. 22.

|| Vakyasudha. 5. also Bhagvad Geeta. Ch. III. 42. $ Vakyasudha. 20.

¶ Bhagvad Geeta Ch. X. 42.

occurs a Schism in the relationship of *Brahma* with *Jagat*. There are those* on the one hand who believe that the universe is Brahma, in this sense that the inexhaustible Brahma converts itself into the universe, while there are those† on the other hand, who maintain that inasmuch as we know nothing of the universe *per se*, save our consciousness of its existence, and that inasmuch as the allpervading and uniform Brahma can hardly admit of changes either physical, moral, or intellectual in its eternal substance, the universe is Brahma itself in the sense that all the so-called nonBrahma phenomena are but the result of that eternal ignorance which binds us for a time and produces these make-believe dreams in a part of the universal Intelligence; or the Platonic Demiurgos. According to the former the *limits* set by human intelligence to the phenomenal universe are futile, whereas according to the latter the whole phenomenal universe reduces itself to a mere dream or illusion. Though apparently fraught with such disastrous consequences, these two doctrines appear on a closer examination to hinge upon nearly the same pivot. Let us look upon the question from another stand-point. The universe which is capable of at best being generalised into Being, must be looked upon as a compact and illimitable whole, free from all differences of *name* and *form*, or *limit*. It is certainly in this sense and this sense alone that the universe is *Brahma*.‡ It is possible thus to perceive that what the one wants to put down in the form of *limits* created by human intelligence, the other wants to supress in the form of *ignorance*. The chief aim of both, either by maintaining the universe to be Brahma transformed, or by annihilating the universe as a mere illusion, is clearly to abolish the distinction between an extra-cosmic creator and his creation. This much being clearly stated, we shall shortly have occasion to discuss the bearing of these two doctrines on

---

* the followers of Vallabha and others.

† the followers of Shankaráchárya.

‡ यथा हि सौम्यैकेन मृत्पिण्डेन सर्वं मृण्मयं विज्ञातं स्याद्वाचारंभणं विकारो नामधेयं....... मृत्तिकेत्येव सत्यम. Chhándogya.

several other important issues. Thus ends our preliminary inquiry into the nature of the First cause and its relation with its Effects—the universe. We have seen how the human mind starting from the vulgar theory of an extra-cosmic Creator soars higher and higher till it loses itself in the essential identity and one-ness of the intelligent cosmos. I might venture to add that it is denied to the mind of man to soar higher still; and the fact that philosophers like Plato and Berkly and Kaut and Hegel have in different countries and at different times arrived at nearly the same conclusion from premises entirely different from the above, greatly adds to the strength of the assertion.

The question next presenting itself for consideration is the one about the nature or relation of evolved sentient life with the universal substance. This question presupposes the existence of a soul in men or rather in things. This is not the place for examining the arguments for and against the existence of such a principle in creation, but it suffices for our purpose to state that all the six principal schools of Aryan philosophy are at one in granting the existence of an intelligent principle or soul of creation. The Naiyayikas and the Vaisheshikes count it among the *dravyas* or substances and look upon it as infinitesimally small and entirely inferior to God or the Supreme Soul in every respect. As the Sànkhyas deny the existence of all intelligence existing apart from matter, they have no theory about the *nature* of this intelligence; but they hold that every atom of matter is full of life and every phenomenon of life implies matter. Patanjali and Jaimini appear from their way of attaining eternal bliss to countenance the theory of a Supreme Being as existing apart, and commanding service from, the Inferior soul. The opinion of the Vedánta on this point is but too clear. Every phenomenon passing under the name of soul is but the individualisation of the universal substance by ignorance* or accidents which being clearly understood and therefore dispelled, the residuum is the one

* Bhagvad Geeta Ch. XIII. 22. also Ch. II. 20. also Ch, XV. 7. 16.

unique and never-changing *sat, chit, ánand.* We see that this is the natural corollary of the Vedantic theory about the universe, and more clearly of the *Vivarta* theory than the *Parináma* one. Aryan scholars are divided in their opinion upon the *Sutras* of Vyas (the best authority on the Vedanta) countenancing the one doctrine or the other. There are some who are inclined to believe, with Mr. H. T. Colebrooke,* that the natural meaning of the sutras points to the *Parináma* doctrine, whereas we have the able and exhaustive commentary of Shaukaràchàrya pointing all the other way. Be that however as it may. We are compelled to resist the temptation of carrying out both these doctrines to their legitimate consequences, and to postpone their consideration once more a little further on.

The question that immediately concerns us most is the obvious one of the usefulness of all this intricate metaphysical discussion; and to it we must therefore address ourselves. The mind of man has been ever trying with varied success to obtain happiness—that which is good or The Good. Our inquiry divides itself at the beginning into two minor aspects: first whether there is any evil as such in the world, and secondly if there is, how to account for its presence and get rid of it. If evil emanates from God, he can hardly be good and omnipotent at the same time. Aryan philosophy holds that, in the nature of the godhead there is no evil whatever, but what accrues as such to men is from causes set in action by themselves or by the law of *Karma*. The Vedántins maintain that we raise idle distinctions between happiness and misery and the like only so long as that *ignorance* which is the cause of this dream of the world, has not been suppressed. Having thus seen that in the nature of things there is no evil, we are confronted by the query, what is Happiness? In the objective world, every thing is overshadowed by futility; and so also in the subjective world of the mind. Happiness could hardly rest in living according to the dictates of our senses

---

* Essays on the religion of the Hindus Vol. II. Vedanta

or even the impulses of our mind. That absolute happiness, that complete bliss, in which not a single particle of any countrary feeling could find place is impossible, unless we *realise*, and live the life of, universal Brahma. Such happiness, says the Vedàntin, commences in—knowledge—knowledge of one's own self *—and its communion, we might say, with the so-called universal essence. "There can" justly remarks Professor. Bain† "be no very great happiness without paying regard to Individuality;" —Individuality we must add, as constituting but a part and parcel of, and therefore utimately losing itself in, the universal Individuality‡ of Brahma. The cause of pain is the *manas* made up of *chitta* and *Ahankára*—or the mental states of taking an interest in objective pursuits, and attributing the performance of actions to one's self.§ If the mind can be suppressed, if the eternal *A'tman* of men can see itself every where, all idea of evil or pain must vanish—all must shine as one illustrious whole made up of knowledge and bliss. In dreamless sleep say the Vedántins we are conscious of nothing unpleasant; whereas we go on feeling pleasure and pain as we advance towards wakefulness. This is explained by saying that the *Ahankára* (Personality) in men is during that kind of sleep *en rapport* with the universal *Ahankara*; and that while approaching towards wakefulness it is memory that binds this Ahankára to its former associations and makes it feel pleasure and pain &c. Hence they infer that *Ahankára* and memory, or the *Manas*, is the cause of pain, and that the state of *Brahma Samádhi* (unity with Branhma) is something similar to, or beyond, dreamless sleep—viz. a kind of conscious sleep (*Turya Avasthá* = fourth state) a' trance full of the ever-lasting consciousness of *Sat*, *Chit* and *Ananda*.|| One who has attained to this condition stands above all the vulgar emotions of this world, is never bound by

---

* Bhagvad Geeta. Ch. IV. 38. 39. Ch. V. 21. 24.

† Mental science-apsendix P. 83.

‡ Bhagvad Geeta. Ch. VI. 29. 31. Chap. XIV. 2. Ch. XVIII. 20.

§ idem Ch. III. 27.

|| Vakya Sudha and Panchadasi and Bhagvad-Geeta Ch. II. 19.

the law of *karma*, and is never born and reborn in the ordinary sense of the term.† Thus we are able to arrive at a clear comprehension of what is conceived to be the ideal of absolute happiness by Vedántic philosophy.

It now remains to examine the bearing of this and other Aryan theories of happiness on human conduct, and to grasp if possible the best way of approaching such an ideal. Having once determined the goal of human efforts, we can very easily decide upon the merits of any given piece of human conduct. Though in setting up Happiness as the ultimate end of human action, the Vedántins appear to countenance the expediency-philosophy of Utilitarianism, there is this important difference between the two, that, while the one looks forward to perfection, to the good, in the nature of event; the other looks to the good in the circumstances or order of events. According to the one, that only will be expedient which is good; according to the other, that only will be good which is expedient. While thus the Vedántic code of morals asserts its superiority over one of the most important modern theories of ethics, it maintains its high position even among the theories deducible from the other phases of Aryan philosophy. Let us for a moment try to analyse the moral standard of those who abide by the theory of an extra- cosmic Supreme-Being requiring strict obedience at our hands to his commands. There is the same difference between the conduct of the the deist and the Vedántin as between the conduct of one carrying out the orders of an intelligent master and another following the dictates of his own convictions. The distinction between one's self and the rest of the world creates a kind of corresponding difference, it may be sometimes even direct opposition, between one's moral conduct towards either. What holds good for himself may sometimes not hold good for the world at large and *vice versa*. When we add to these two, a governor supervising the whole and listening to our prayers, we

---

* Bhagvad-Geeta Ch. VI. also भिद्यतेहृदयग्रंथिश्छिद्यंते सर्वसंशयाः क्षीयंतेचास्यकर्माणितस्मिन्दृष्टेपरावरे ॥ MANDUKA-UPANISHAD.

set up a third standard of morality at times unifying the other two in itself, at times jarring with all. The highest moral ideal conceivable results from looking upon the universe as nothing apart from the individual self and *vice versa*, and from *feeling* that the individual is but a sentient fibre of the intelligent whole, rising with its rise and falling, so to say, with its fall.* It now follows as a natural consequence that one who thus lives in Brahma and of Brahma, breathes as it were in conformity with the universal breath of intelligent nature, and hardly collects any store of causes capable of producing pleasure or pain. In other words, the law of *Karma* does not bind an ascetic who thus identifies his individuality with the universal totality.† The Vedántic doctrine we thus see is prolific of good results in every department of human knowledge, and leads to right conduct, right action, right understanding and right everything. This, however, is far too ideal a standard, an Utilitarian might retort, to be of any use in practical life. Before dismissing this theory on such a feeble ground as this, we must look around us in the department of Morals, Intelligence, nay even Physics and see how many will be the ideals after which human beings are running in mad eagerness with very poor success. And is the world, we may ask, a whit the worse for having done so? We shall best answer this argumemt in the words of a celebrated philosopher. "It is true that pure rectitude prescribes a system of things far too good for men as they are; it is not less true that mere expediency does not of itself tend to establish a system of things any better than that which exists. While absolute morality owes to expediency the checks which prevent it from rushing into utopian absurdities; expediency is indebted to absolute morality for all stimulus to improvement. Granted that we are chiefly interested in ascertaining what is *relatively right*, it still follows that we must first consider what is *absolutely right*; since the one conception presupposes the other."‡

---

* Bhagvad Geeta. Ch. VI. 29—32.

† Idem. Ch. IV. 37. Ch. V. 7.

‡ H. Spencer's Essay. "Prison Ethics."

The last point to be considered is the *mode* of attaining to the highest end in view. It goes without saying that the *modus operandi* must vary with the character of the end proposed. The *Vedas* abound chiefly in hymns and prayers useful at the performance of Sacrifices of different kinds. In other words, these sacred books enjoin what is popularly called *Upàsana* (devotion) and *Karma* (the performance of Vedic-rites). The path of pure knowledge (called *Dnyán Márga*) is indicated at the end of the *Vedas* (in the Vedánta) as the essence of the whole teaching. This being the case, philosophers are at once divided among themselves as to the best mode of attaining *Moksha.* There are some who strictly follow the course of devotion ; there are some who stick to the line of knowledge ; while there are some again who pass to the latter through the former. The Naiyayikas and the Vaisheshikas, inasmuch as they are believers in the doctrine of a personal Creator, hold up the efficacy of prayer, and seek for absolution in devotion to the Supreme Being. The Sánkhyas, on the other hand, having no God to satisfy, hold that *Purush* unites with *Prakriti* for the exhaltation of the latter to its highest state, and for its own enjoyment. The attributes of *Prakriti* are three in number : *Sattva* (purity), *Rajas* (foulness), and *Tamas* (darkness) ; and it works its way to creation through an interaction of these *gunas.* It is by living according to the law of the highest attribute of *Prakriti* viz. *Sattva,* that we attain to the highest happiness or *moksha*, inasmuch as all misery is but the offspring of the other two. The various marks of these *gunas* are therefore enumerated with a view to enforce the observance of *Sattva* guna alone in supersession of the other two. This, no doubt, is an advance upon the theory of a personal God, listening to our prayers and dealing out the fruits of our actions accordingly. Patanjali advances a step further and prescribes a number of rules for the guidance of the mind and the body with the same end as the Sánkhyas in view. He seems however to countenance the theory of an extra-cosmic Supreme Being by whose grace we are able to obtain absolution. His system of *Yoga* (Union or communion with the Supreme Being) leads through the attainment of certain occult powers called the eight *Siddhis*, to that state of the mind or soul wherein there is all light and bliss, and whereby the Yogee is supposed to defy the laws of the universe as understood by ordinary beings, even death. This *yoga* has been viewed by later writers from two different stand-points: and this circumstance has led to its division into *Hatha* (physical,) and *Rája* (mental) *Yoga*.* Though the end to be achieved in either instance is the same, viz, the union of the mind with the Supreme Soul—one holds it possible to attain to it through several physical postures regulating the breath and through it the mind; the other addresses itself directly to the mind and its regulation. The Sánkhya and the Yoga have thus reduced what other religions mention simply by way of advice, to a regular science, and have thus far remained as it were in a sense between *Upásana* and *Dnyán* or *Nyáya* and *Vedánta*. The *purva mimánsá* or *mimánsâ* proper, the work of *Jaimini*, is devoted chiefly to the interpreration of Vedic texts and their bearings on formal religion and philosophy. It declares the necessity of observing all the rites and ceremonies enjoined by the *Vedas* and as it were indirectly inculcates that the way to the knowledge (*Dnyán*) leading to *Moksha* lies through *Karma*. The *Uttara Mimánsá* or *Vedánta* proper, the work of *Bádaráyan Vyás*, is devoted entirely to a discussion of philosophy and metaphysics illustrated by quotations from the *Upanishads*, and the *Vedas*. As has been already remarked more than once, there is much of discussion as to whether the *Sutras* of *Vyás*,

---

* *Ha* Means the sun a symbol for the breath called *Prána*, and *tha* means the Moon—a symbol for the breath called *Apána*. The union of the two is necessary for producing the state leading to *Samádhi* or trance. Hence *Hatha yoga* means the Science of regulating the breath for this purpose. The word Rájyoga is probably derived from the root Ráj to shine alluding in the present instance to the luminosity of the Soul or *Atman* so often described in the Shrutis. Rája yoga, another word for *Samadhi* or trance, which means the merging of the *mind* in the *soul*, may therefore mean concentration or union with the illustrious (Soul or Brahma).

advocate the *Parinàma* or the *Vivarta* theory of evolution. Leaving the decision of this much-disputed point to abler hands, we must for tho present content ourselves with examining the bearing of both the doctrines on the main issue of our inquiry. The *Parinámavàdi* as well as the *Vivartavàdi* are both at one in declaring *moksha* as the realization of the unity of *Brahma* and *Jiva.* The one however lays great stress on divesting our mind of its propensity to encircle things with a limit of its own creation, whereas the other, reducing the whole Universe to a mere illusion, aims at dispelling it from our limited vision. Both aim at that qualitative extension of the mind which will cover the same ground as universal *A'tman,* and leave no *residuum* behind. The one tries to reach this end by extending the mind through *devotion,* the other by dispelling *illusion* through ascetic practices. The one may be said to advocate the theory of universal love from individual love,—the other universal real knowledge, from individual real understanding. This is the opposition between *Bhakti* and *Dnyán* as philosophically understood, an oppsition that has led to differences and disputes, sects and creeds without end. We however are inclined to look upon this distinction as rather verbal than real in its character. So far as the end in view remains the same, the means may be left to adapt themselves to the requisites of time and circumstances. At times it may be more convenient to lead the mind to the state of universal extention by first nourishing any one of its higher propensities, say love ; at others it may be easy to achieve the same result by encouraging any other propensity, say asceticism and knowledge. But such a circumstance hardly affords in our opinion any solid ground for any hostile opposition between sect and sect or religion and religion.

The Vedántic process then of attaining to this state of Brahma generally described as *Rájayoga* is purely mental, and deals entirely with rules for restraining the mind. Shankaràchàrya, the advocate of the *Vivartaváda* while accepting the cosmogony of the *Sánkhyas* and the *yoga* system of *Patanjali,* considerably improved upon both. He abolished the idle distinction between inseparable *Purusha* and *Prakriti* as an inconvenient bar in the way of any action for *Moksha* as such, and declared that the whole universe was all *Purusha*, or *Brahma*.* Further, perceiving the inutility of physical *Yoga* towards the annihilation of the *mind*, he set up the practice of mental yoga as both practical and easy. According to his teaching it will be pure moral cowardice on the one hand to shrink from one's duties in life, and sheer unmanliness on the other to be engrossed in, or unnerved by, the good or evil results of our necessary functions.

If we correctly grasp the character and nature of the grand idea, which we are pursuing every moment with all our might —viz happiness, three-fourths, nay even the whole of our miseries will reduce themselves to nothing. " Having found the object to be made happy in the Self, it becomes necessary to examine its nature so as to determine how to make it happy.. ......As the investigation into the true elements of happiness advances, a vory inportant fact becomes apparent from our conception of time. We see that the personality, the aspirant for happiness, has itself such a constitution as to be unable to exist without change in consciousness, and that exist it must. That which is, can never absolutely cease to be; no relatiouship can be legitmately postulated between a thing and its utter negation. Therefore the scheme of happiness, which the personality sets up in igorrnce of its own nature, must be given up for its true happiness. In order to be truly happy, the personality has to realise its own perpetual changefulness, and the result of such realization will be the surrender of the desire for the permanence of any particular state of its existence, a desire springing from ignorance of its own nature............To be supremely happy we must renounce all desire for happiness as the result of our work, but find it in the work itself."† Thus

---

* Compare the Purusha Sukta. Rig. Veda.

† The Theosophist, Vol. VI. No. 6. compare also Bhagvad-Geeta Ch. II. 47. 48.

perceiving the necessity of determining the elements of happiness, we naturally arrive at that stage of Rájyoga which is called *Viveka* (discrimination). Inasmuch as happiness does not exist outside the ego or *A'tma*, and as a further analysis of one's self leads one to see everything in and of it, a distinction more imaginary than real is drawn at the beginning for the practical guidance of the neophyte, between things which are A'tma, and those that are not-A'tma. When the beginner thus goes on dissecting the nature of things and studying the various phases of his own *ego*, he naturally becomes saturated with a sense of universal change which pervades everything, so much so, that even the desire for the permanence of any particular state never enters his heart. This is the second step generally known as *Virága* (disgust). Then follow six other subordinate steps first among which is *Shama*. When the student is convinced of the futility of all desire, he applies himself naturally to the study of the higher psychological aspects of his changeful consciousness. As a result of this constant application he becomes estranged from the objects of sense, both subjective and objective, and directs his whole attention to a contemplation of the one uniform existence of change which he is intent upon understanding in its supperior aspects (*Dama*). It follows then that, if the student clearly realises the progress that he is expected to have made by this time, his mind (*Vritti*) disengages itself from every thing but the object he has in view. This state is the one (*Uparati*) which is followed as a corollary by the fifth called *Titiksha* or putting up with the so-called pleasures and pains of the world with patience and without any excitement. When this stage is reached, the *Ahankára* or the personality of the student begins to lose itself completely in the universal intelligence he is contemplating, and it is faith (*Shraddhá*) in his own convictions as well as in the words of advanced interpreters of science that leads to a strong and unchanging attachment (*Samádhána*) of his faculties to Brahma, the principle and essence of the Cosmos. When these stages are passed, he is said to be a *mumukshu* one desirous of knowing the real nature of the phenomena of duality or non-Brahma, viz. *Ahankára,* and the physical bonds consequnt upon its hold. This course of training leads to the fixity of his mind which then "stands like the jet of a lamp that burns steadily in a place protected from the slightest breeze." While thus studying his "ego" he reaches a stage in which his senses both objective and subjective, see nothing else but the Divine Intelligence.—Brahma—wherever it is directed.* "He alone obtains the state of eternal bliss whose heart maintains its steadiness under the flux (and efflux) of (all kinds of) desires; like the ocean which, though constantly receiving fresh additions of water, remains firmly confined within its natural limits." "Such a one" says Krishna "gets perfect quiet and not he whom every little breeze of pleasure or pain wafts hither and thither."† It is never the object of the *Geeta* or any other system of Rájyoga to dissuade any man from the duties of his legitimate sphere; for, says Krishna even life itself which is supposed to be necessary for accomplishing all this *knowledge,* can hardly become possible without the performance of its natural functions. What is required, and what follows as a natural consequence of the said course of training, is freedom from the calculation of the results of our necessary actions. It will be evident from this rough outline of the elements of *Rájyoga,* which will be found described at full length in the Bhagvad Geeta as well as in the two small works which follow, that the object which Hathayoga wants to accomplish is here placed within the reach of every willing student without a renunciation of the world and its responsibilities as required by the preliminary course of Hathayoga-training.

* Vákyasudhá. † Bhagavad Geeta chap. II. 70.

SHRI VAKYA SUDHA

OR

THE PHILOSOPHY OF SUBJECT AND OBJECT

THE ETERNAL ATMAN.

I. Form is the object, and the eye is the subject of all our objective perception; the eye, however, is cognised by the mind, (the phenomena of) which again are objects of perception to the ever present subjective *Atman* which in the series can never be the object of any ultimate perception.*

II. The eye, perceiving various forms, such as blue, yellow, large, small, short, long, etc., remains all the same—ever unaffected and uniformly one. [The rule of perception, implied is this: those are *objects* of perception (दृश्य), which possess the property of presenting themselves in *many* forms; and those are *subjects* of perception (द्रष्टा), with regard to any the same perception, which remain *one and unaffected* by the forms of the objects cognised.]

III. The keenness, slowness, or blindness of sight imply various properties in the eye (present the eye under *many forms*), all cognised by the mind, which remains *one and un-*

* Compare.

कर्तारंचक्रियांतद्वत् व्याहृतविषयानपि ।
स्फोरयेदेकयत्नेन योऽसौसाक्ष्यत्रचिद्वपुः ॥
ईक्षेशृणोमिजिघ्रामि स्वादयामिस्पृशाम्यहं ।
इतिभासयतेसर्वं नृत्यशालास्थदीपवत् ।
पंचदशी ॥ १० ॥ ९ ॥ १० ॥

affected. The same may, by parity of reasoning, be said of the other organs of sense, as the ear, the skin, &c.

IV. The mind again is an *object* of perception: the *Atman* cognises the whole phenomena of the mind, viz., desire, imagination, doubt, belief, disbelief, shame, intelligence, fear, etc.; remaining itself unique and unaffected.

(The *Atman* cannot be assumed to be the *object* of any further perception; for such a theory would involve us in confusion *ad infinitum.* Nor is the absurdity that the *Atman* itself is both the *subject and object* of perception at all tenable. The *Atman* therefore shines by its own lustre and illumines all other objects of perception.)

V. This *(Atman)* never appears or disappears, never waxes or wanes. It shines by its own light and enlightens the whole without any (exterior) help.

The substance implied is this: that, which does not shine by its own light, is subject to transformation, as *Ahankára* (egoism). Again, *Atman* enlightens the whole as साक्षि-द्रष्टा and is therefore not subject to change; for that, which does not shine *independently* of *visible matter* (जड), is not free from change (निर्विकार) as *egoism,* etc. Thus *Atman,* being beyond all change (निर्विकार) and shining by its own lustre (स्वयंप्रकाश), ever remains the *subject* (द्रष्टा) of all knowledge, and can never be the *object* of any ultimate perception. This subjective *Atman* is thus proved to be *Paramatman.* It is the one implied by त्वम् in the *Sruti* तत्त्वमसि; and is one with the परब्रह्म implied by तत् in the same. Though in this manner *Atman* and *Paramatman* are one and the same, it is necessary to dispel the *ignorance* which interferes with the realisation of their unity.

THE LINGADEHA.

VI. A reflection of the *Atman* in *Buddhi* enkindles it (makes the substantially *material Buddhi* believe itself to be entire *spirit*). This *Buddhi* is of two sorts: *Ahankara* and

Antaskarana. (The *doer*, the *subject* of all action is *Ahankára*; and the *Antaskarana* or *Manas* is its instrument.)*

VII. The unity of *Ahankára* with the reflecuion of *Atman* is as inseparable as that of a heated ball of iron with the fire that heats it. *Ahankára* identifies itself with the external physical body also, which thereupon becomes spiritualized: believes itself to be all spirit.†

VIII. The identification of *Ahankara* with the reflection of *Atman*, with the physical external shell, and with the *subject* of all knowledge—*Atman*,—is respectively *inherent* (is from the beginning of *Ahankára*), through *actions* (*i. e.*, कर्म as those performed during the waking state), and through *ignorance* (अविद्या).

IX. Of these three, the inherent identification of *Ahankara* with the reflection of *Atman* is never destroyed; whereas that with the other two is destroyed by the exhaustion of कर्म, and by knowledge respectively.

X. When *Ahankára* merges into original ignorance, sleep is induced, and the physical body (स्थूलदेह), which appeared with spirit by its identification with *Ahankára* in the waking state, becomes as it were lifeless. When *Ahankara* is half awake, the state produced in the astral body (लिंगदेह) is the one called dream; and when it is wide awake, the state produced is

---

* Compare.

" Antaskarana is the path of communion between soul and body entirely disconnected with the former; existing with, belonging to, and dying with the body."—*Editor's note, Theosophist, Vol. IV, No. 11, p. 268.*

अहमित्यभिमंताप: कर्तासीतस्यसाधनं ।
मनस्तस्याक्रियेअंत र्बहिर्वृत्तिक्रमोत्थिते ॥
अंतर्मुखाहमित्येषा वृत्ति:कर्तारमुल्लिखेत् ।
बहिर्मुखेदमित्येशा बाह्यंवस्त्विदमुल्लिखेत् ॥पंचदशी॥१०॥६॥७॥

† Compare.

अहंवृत्तौचिदाभास: कामक्रोधादिकेषुच ।
संव्याप्यवर्ततेतप्ते लोहेवान्हिर्यथातथा ॥ पंचदशी ॥८॥१८॥

sleeplessness or waking. (Thus all कर्म is dependent on *Ahankara* which, when merged into universal *Ahankara* as in sleep, gives rise to none.)*

XI. The *Antaskarana*, identifying itself with the reflection of *Atman*, creates, in dream, the impressions (वासना) necessary for the action of such कर्म as affect the astral body (सूक्ष्मदेह), and, in the waking state, the *objective* realities (our interest in those realities) necessary for the enjoyment of such कर्म as affect the physical form (स्थूलदेह).

XII. The astral body (*Linga deha*), which is made up of *Manas* and *Ahankara*, is essentially material in its nature. It experiences the three states of waking, dreaming and sleeping, as undergoes also the transformations of death and birth.†

MAYA AND ITS POWERS.

XIII. Having described how the लिंगदेह is the basis of all our ordinary intercourse, it is proposed to examine the genesis of this देह from *Maya* or illusion. *Maya has* two powers. *Vikshepa* and *Avarana*, of which *Vikshepa* or *extension* evolves the whole world, beginning from the लिंगदेह to the all-embracing universe, from *Brahma*.

XIV. This evolution may be described as the attributing

---

* "The Vedantic philosophy teaches as much as Occult philosophy that our *Monad*, during its life on earth as a triad (7th, 6th, and 5th principles), has, besides the condition of pure intelligence, three conditions; viz., waking, dreaming and *sushupti*—a state of dreamless sleep—from the stand-point of terrestrial conception; of real actual soul-life from the occult stand-point. While man is either dreamlessly, profoundly asleep or in trance-state, the triad (spirit soul and the mind) enters into perfect union with the *Paramatman*—the Supreme Universal soul":—*Editor's Note, Theosophist. Vol. IV., No.* 11, *p.* 267.

† क्रमाद्विच्छिद्य विच्छिद्य जायन्ते वृत्तयोऽखिलाः ।
सर्वा अपि विलीयंते सुप्तमुर्छासमाधिषु । पंचदशी ॥८॥२०॥

Compare

शोकहर्षभयक्रोधलोभमोहस्पृहादयः ।
अहंकारस्य दृश्यन्ते जन्ममृत्युश्च नात्मनः । आत्मगीता ।

name and form to that *Brahma* which is all existence, all knowledge, and all joy —like the attributing of name and form as फेन (foam), तरंग (waves), बुद्बुद (bubbles), &c., to the waters of the ocean.

XV. That is another power of *Maya-Avarana* or *immersion* —which, as the cause of this world, throws, as it were, the veil of reality over the unreal internal distinction between the object and the subject of knowledge, as also over the external one between *Brahma* and creation.

XVI. That लिंगशरीर, which shines by the reflection of the immovable *Atman*, the witness of all phenomena and noumena, and which is, as it were, one with the स्थूलशरीर, the external shell, becomes (by the force of *Avarana Shakti)* जीव in our ordinary life, *i. e.*, is for our ordinary intercourse termed जीव or soul.

XVII. By the force of the same *Avarana*, the witness of all, the कूटस्थब्रह्म, also shines as if it were जीव. The distinction between जीव and the साक्षी being clearly grasped (by ज्ञान), this illusion melts away.

XVIII. Similarly *Brahma* appears manipulated into many forms by the force of that power (*Avarna*) which covers the distinction (unreal distinction) between creation and *Brahma.*

XIX. Here also, by the destruction of *Avarana,* the distinction between *Brahma* and creation becomes so far clear as to enable us to attribute all change (विकार), viz., name and form, to the latter and not to the former.

XX. All intercourse implies five attributes and no more: existence (सत्); intelligence (चित्); love (आनंद); form (रूप); and name (नाम). The first three of these represent the all-pervading *Brahma*, and the last two the unreal *Jagat* (world, creation).

XXI. In the elements, *Akasa*, *Vayu*, *Tejas*, *Apas*, and *Prithvi*; as also in the different degrees of creation, gods, birds, animals, and men;—the *Sat, Chit,* and, *Ananda,* are ever one and uniform—that which differs is simply the form and the name.

THE COURSE OF RELISING THE BRAHMA TATVA.

(Samadhi or concentration).

XXII. Neglectnig therefore the unreal creation consistiug of mere name and form. (abstracting all one's interest from the objects. of this world), one (desirous of final absolution) should meditate on the *Satchidanand Brahma*, and should ever practise mental as well as physical concentration.

XXIII. Mental concentration is of two kinds :—*Savikalpaka* and *Nirvikalpaka*; the former again is of two kinds: *Drishyanuviddha* and *Shabdanuviddha*.

XXIV The दृश्यानुविध्यसविकल्पसमाधिः is the meditation of the subjective *Atman*, as the witness of the mental world—the passions, desires, &c., arising in the *Manas*.

XXV The शब्दानुविध्यसविकल्पसमाधि is the fixing one's mind on "I am(that) *Brahma*" which is (described in the Vedás) as self-existent, eternal, all-intelligence and love, self-illumined and unique in itself.

XXVI That is *Nirvakalpa Samadhi* in which, through the ecstacy of the pleasure consequent upon the knowledge of one's self, the *mental* (दृश्य) as well as *the nominal* (शब्द) are both overlooked: and (the mind) stands like the jet of a lamp burning in a place protected from the slightest breeze.*

XXVII The separation in any external object of sight, of name and form, from its original *substratum, sat*, is *external phenomenal* (दृश्यानुविध्य) concentration (like the *internal mental* one des- cribed before).

XXVIII The meditation on the one, unique, and *Satchidanand Brahma* (described in the Shruties), as the only reality in this universe, is *external, nominal* (शब्दानुविध्य) concentration.

---

* Compare

यथादीपोनिवातस्थो नेंगतेसोपमास्मृता ।

योगिनोयतचित्तस्य युंजतोयोगमात्मनः । भगवद्गीता ॥६॥१९॥

XXIX The third *(Nirv ikalpa Samadhi)* concentration is like the one described before, cessation of all thought except the enjoyment of the one eternal pleasure arising from the experience of the universal *Paramatman* (which thus proves to be one with the subjective *Atman* shown as the subject of *internal Nirvikalpa Samadhi)*. Every one should devote the whole of his time to these six kinds of *Samadhis.*

XXX The egoism in the physical body being annihilated in this manner, and he *Universal Atman* being thoroughly realised, wherever the mind of the ascetic is directed, there it *naturally* loses itself into one or other of these *Samadhis.*

XXXI The identification of the phenomenal as well as the noumenal with the one eternal unchangeable *Brahma* being realised, the knot (of the unreal identification of *ha Ankára* with *Atman)* of the heart is at once split open; all doubts vanish in a minute; and all *Karma (Sanchita, Prarabdha,* and *Kriyamana)* is destroyed in the very bud.* [*Karma* does not affect the absolved ascetic. *Parabdha* or that part of *Sanchita,* of which this life is an evolute, runs its course and ends with this life; *Kriyamana,* or that, which is being done at present in obedience to *Prarabdha,* has no stability in as much as its storehouse is destroyed by the destruction of *Lingadeha*; and *Sanchita,* (or that portion of past *Karma,* which has not yet borne fruit, plus the results of present *Karma* which are to bear their fruit) also has no room for its operation; for the *Lingadeha,* through which all its future manifestations on the platform of our physical frame become possible, has no existence.]†

* This Shruti is taken from the Manduka Upanishad, with which compare.

यदासर्वेप्रभिद्यन्ते हृदयग्रंथयस्त्विति ।

कामाग्रंथिस्वरूपेण व्याख्यातावाक्यशेषतः । पंचदशी ॥६॥२६०॥

† Compare.

ज्ञानाग्निःसर्वकर्माणि भस्मसात्कुरुतेऽर्जुन । भगवद्गीता ।

आत्मानंचाद्विजानीया दयमस्मीतिपुरुषः ।

किमिच्छन्कस्यकामाय शरीरमनुसंज्वरेत् ॥ पंचदशी ॥७॥१॥

The unity of Atman and Parmatman or Brahma.

XXXII *Jiva* is of three kinds : the first is that portion (अवच्छिन्न) of *Brahma* which is limited (by *Avidya* and *Ahankàra*); the second is the reflection of the *Atman* into the *Lingadeha*; and the third is the one imagined as active in dreams. Of these three, it is the first only which has any real existence. (If जीव is only a limited portion of *Brahma*, how can it be *Brahma* itself? With this doubt in view it is said) :—

XXXIII The limit (in *Brahma*) is simply imaginary (since it is destructible by the merging of *Ahankàra* and *Avidya* into *Brahma* by proper (knowledge) and the *real thing* is that which is limited (viz., *Brahma*). It is assumed to be *Jiva* only by imagination, but by nature it is (one with) *Brahma*.

XXXIV It is the unity of this imaginary (अवच्छिन्न) *Jiva* with *Brahma* that is inculcated in such phrases as तत्त्वमसि (in the *Chhandogya Upanishad*); and not with the other *Jivas*.*

XXXV In *Brahma* exists *Máya* in its two aspects of विक्षेप and आवृत्ति, which, covering the unique unchangeable *Brahma*, attributes the universe and the soul to it (evolves the universe from it.)

XXXVI The reflection of *Atman* in *Buddhi* is the *Jiva* which enjoys the fruits of its *Karma*; and this transitory universe is the thing that is enjoyed by it.

ननिरोधोनचोत्पत्तिर्न बध्धोनचसाधकः ।
नमुमुक्षुर्नवैमुक्त इत्येषापरमार्थता ॥ पंचदशी ॥ ८ ॥ ७१ ॥

* Compare.

एकमेवाद्वितीयंस न्नामरूपविवर्जितम् ।
सृष्टेःपुराऽधुनाप्यस्य तादृक्त्वंतदितीर्यते ॥
श्रोतुर्देहेन्द्रियातीतं वस्त्वत्रत्वंपदेरितम् ।
एकताग्राह्यतेऽसीति तदैक्यमनुभूयताम् ॥

पंचदशी ॥ ६ ॥ ७ ॥ ८ ॥

XXXVII. The duality (of *Jiva* and *Jagat*) which exists from time immemorial* has any reality only till the time† of final absolution. It is therefore useful only so far as our ordinary intercourse is concerned.

(This duality is of two kinds: इश्वरकृत and जीवकृत; the destruction of the latter is necessary for absolution,‡ for the name and form given to the objects of this world is a creation, purely mental and obstructive to absolution, as such.§)

XXXVIII. The sleep, which, in its two aspects of *Viskshepa* and *Avarana*, is the quality of reflected *Atman*, covers the whole of *Jiva* and *Jagat* (in sleep) and creates (in dream) new ones in their place.

(These are called the प्रातिभासिक *Jiva* and *Jagat*. The comparison implied is this:—Just as sleep resides in the चिदाभास, *Máya* resides, as it were, potentially in ब्रह्म; and, as sleep covers the व्यावहारिकजीव and जगत् and creates the प्रातिभासिक ones in their place, so *Maya* covers ब्रह्म and evolves from it the व्यावहारिक जीव and जगत् instead.)

---

* प्रकृतिंपुरुषंचैव विध्यनादीउभावपि ॥ भगवद्गीता ॥

† चोद्यंवापरिहारोवा ।क्रियतांद्वैतभाषया ।
अद्वैतभाषयाचोद्यं नास्ति । पंचदशी ।

‡ अतःसर्वस्यजीवस्य बंधकृन्मानसंजगत् ॥ पंचदशी ॥४॥३९॥
जीवन्मुक्तेःपराकाष्ठा जीवद्वैतविवर्जनात् ।
लभ्यतेऽसावतोऽत्रेदमीशद्वैताद्विवेचितम् ।पंचदशी ॥ ४ ॥ ६१ ॥

§ मूषासिक्तंयथाताम्रंतान्निभंजायतेतथा ।
रूपादीन्व्याप्नुवच्चित्तं तन्निभंदृश्यतेध्रुवम् ।
सर्वार्थव्यंजकत्वाध्धीरर्थाकाराप्रदृश्यते ।
पंचदशी ॥ ४ ॥ २८ ॥ २९ ॥

XXXIX. As these (*Jiva* and *Jagat*) appear real only during the time of their existence, (*i. e.* in dream) they are called प्रातिभासिक or imaginary: for they are never felt in any other dream after one is awakened from the original dream in which they were experienced. (The previous illustration is thus carried to its legitimate and logical result. As the प्रातिभासिक जीव and जगत् are real only till the dream is broken, so also are the व्यावहारिक जीव and जगत् real only till the spell of *Màya* is broken by ज्ञान; and, also as the व्यावहारिक is one and unchangeable in the प्रातिभासिक creation, so is परब्रह्म in the व्यावहारिक creation. Thus the proposition enunciated in verse 37 is established.)

XL. The प्रातिभासिक जीव believes the प्रातिसिक जगत् to be real whereas the व्यावहारिकजीव knows both of them to be false.

XLI. So does the व्यावहारिक जीव believe the व्यावहारिक जगत् to be real; but the पारमार्थिकजाव (ब्रह्म) knows both of them to be false. (This व्यावहारिक जगत् exists only so long as व्यावहारिक जीव exists. Both are therefore unreal to the पारमार्थिकजीव. In sleep, as also at the time of *Pralaya*, both these disappear, *Brahma* alone sustaining; so also in those who are जीवन्मुक्त, absolved even while living.)

XLII. The *Páràmárthika Jiva* knows itself to be one with *Brahma*, and sees nothing apart from it, for every thing that it sees besides, is seen through unreality.

XLIII. As sweetness, fluidity, coolness and other qualities of water, having manifested themselves in the waves that surge on its bosom, appear also in the foam that plays on the surface of the waves;

XLIV. So do the सत्, चित् and आनंद—, which are inherent in the परमात्मन्, the witness of all—appear in the व्यावहारिक जगत् and, through it, in the प्रातिभासिकजगत् also. (Vide verse No. 20.)

XLV. On the disappearance of foam, its qualities, fluidity, &c., merge into its source, the wave; and, on the disappearance of the latter, its qualities again merge into its source, water, and remain there as before.

XLVI. So, on the dissolution of the *imaginary* जीव its constituents (सत्, चित्, आनंद) flow into its source, the *ordinary* जीव, on whose dissolution again, all these—the residuum—flow into the source, whence everything emanated—the परमात्मन्, Universal Spirit—witness of all.*

---

* यद्यद्रूपादिकल्पेत बुध्यातत्तत्प्रकाशयन् ।
तस्यतस्यभवेत्साक्षी स्वतोवाग्बुध्यगोचरः ।
कथंताद्दृङ्मयाग्राह्य इतिचेन्नैवगृह्यतां ।
सर्वग्रहोपसंशांती स्वयमेवावशिष्यते । पंचदशी ॥२३॥२४॥

DIRECT COGNITION

(OF THE UNITY OF *JIVA* AND *BRAHMA*.)

1. I* bow to Shri Hari†—to Ishwar—the highest happiness, the best instructor, the all-pervading, the one cause (material instrumental as well as final) of the Universe.

2. Hence forward is expounded the course of realising the Invisible, for the easy acquisition of final absolution (from the bonds forged by ignorance-*avidyá*); let those only who have sufficiently prepared themselves for being initiated into the secrets of this Science, by every effort frequently meditate upon the truths herein inculcated.

3. Indifference (1) and the other (3) preliminary qualifications are acquired by the performance of duties peculiar to one's own caste and creed, by austerities, and by propitiating the deities &c.‡

---

* The ego—*the ashuddha jiva* (6th principle) as it were contemplates upon *Ishwar—Brahma*—the creator and yet—the destroyer of all *avidyá*—ignorance, i. e. tries to realise its primal identity with *Brahma*.

† He who by the light of knowledge *takes* away, *melts* away all *avidya*—the common substratum of the three States of sleep dream and waking.

‡ अधिकारीतुविधिवदधीतवेदवेदांगत्वेनापाततोऽधिगताखिलवेदार्थोऽस्मिञ्जन्मनिजन्मान्तरेवाकाम्यानिषिद्धवर्जनपुरःसरंनित्यनैमित्तिकप्रायश्चित्तोपासनानुष्ठानेननिर्गतनिखिलकल्मषतयानितांतनिर्मलस्वांतःसाधनचतुष्टयसम्पन्नःप्रमाताधिकारी ॥

॥ वेदान्तसार ॥ also

मेधावीपुरुषोविद्वानूहापोहविचक्षणः। अधिकार्यात्मविद्यायामुक्तलक्षणलक्षितः ॥
विवेकिनोविरक्तस्यशमादिगुणशालिनः। मुमुक्षोरेवहिब्रह्मजिज्ञासायोग्यतामता ॥

॥ विवेकचूडामणि ॥

4. That is pure Indifference which consists in the loss of all desire for the enjoyments of the senses, beginning from the *Satyaloka* (the highest heaven) to the *Martyaloka* (this world), as for the dung of a crow.

5. The determination that the only eternal and permanent principle of the Cosmos is *Atman* the (*Subject* of all perception), and that every thing else is opposed in its very nature to this *Atman* (i. e., is unpermanent) as being the object* of perception —Such fixed (theoretical) determination, the cause of *Indifference,* is called the Right *knowledge* (2) of objects.

6. Now the effects (3) of *Indifference*:—*Shama, Dama* and four others. The abandonment of all *previous impressions* maturing themselves into tangible effects *now* (*i.e. the controlling* of the *Antaskarana*) is called *Shama* (1); complete restraint over the bent of the external senses (over our bodily acts) is called *Dama* (2).

7. The entire turning away from all objects of sense, the almost voluntary absence of all desire for such objects, is the height of *Uparati* (3); and the patient suffering of all pain or sorrow is the state of happy *Titikshá*‡ (4).

8. Faith in the words of the Upanishads, as well also in the words of those who interpret them—the teachers, (as also, and perhaps chiefly, in one's self)—is called *Shraddhá* (5); the absorption of the mind in the one paramount aim of all exertion—the *Sat*—the Universal *Atman*—(i. e., excessive desire *to know* and *realise* that *Paramatman*; or the utter incapability arising from such a state, of deviating from the right path) is called *Samádhán* (6).

9. When and how shall, oh my Fate, I be free from the bonds of this world—birth and rebirth—this strong and all absorbing desire constitutes the fourth and last of the four preliminary stages—*Desire of Absolution* (4).

---

* Compare Vakya Sudhá 1.

‡ "The cessation of desire, a constant readiness to part with every thing in the world"—Theosphist Vol. V. No. 12. P. 282.

10. One who having passed through the said preliminary stages desires *knowledge* for final absolution must set himself seriously *to think.*

11. Knowledge is not produced by any means other than right thinking; just as the objects of this universe are never perceived but by the help of light.

12. (*a*) Who am I? (*b*) How is this evolved? (*c*) Who is its creator? (*d*) What is the material of which it is made?—This is the form of rational thought.

13. (*a*) I certainly cannot be this body—a mere collection of the various *Tatvas*; nor can I be any one of the senses (for the same reason), I must certainly be something quite apart from both of them:—This is &c.

14. (*b*) Everything emanates from ignorance, and melts away into knowledge; (*c*) the various fancies the *antaskarana* must be the (as understood by us) creator—This is &c.

15. (*d*) The material cause of these two, ignorance and fancy, is the incomprehensibly minute but unique and undecaying everlasting *sat*, just as the earth is the cause of jars etc—This &c.

16. There is no doubt that *I* am one with that supreme *ego*, I am the very ego, which is common to all men, which is unique and one, which is incomprehensibly small, the subject of all perception, the everpresent witness, (seeing everything without the ordinary means of knowledge), the ever existent undecaying spirit:—This &c.

17. The one *Atman*, the ever present Universal spirit—is free from all conditions (as organs of sense &c.), whereas the *Deha* i. e. *lingadeha* or astral body is bound by many*: what ignorance could surpass that of those who confound these two together?

* i. e. 17. The 5 *Prans* + 5 *Dayanendriya* + 5 *Karmendriyas* + Buddhi + Ahankara = 17.

18. The *Atman* is the internal governor of this *deha* which is the governed and therefore external: what ignorance &c.

19. The *Atman* is all conscious Intelligence and all holiness: the deha i. e. the *Sthuladeha* or physical body is all flesh and blood, (i. e. inert) and therefore unclean: what ignorance &c.

20. The *Atman* is the illumination of the Universe and purity itself; the *deha* is all darkness (evolved from ignorance): what ignorance &c.

21. The *Atman* is permanent, eternal and therefore existence itself: whereas the *dehas* are non-eternal (subject to change) and non-existence incarnate: what ignorance &c.

22. That is the self-illuminating power of *Atman*, which enlightens *all* the objects of this Universe: it is not any ordinary light like that of fire or any other thing, which has no power to interfere with the presence of darkness in any the same contiguous place.*

23. It is very strange that people though always talking of this *deha* as something belonging to *me* (the subjective Atman), and therefore apart from He who possesses it, like one seeing a jar of earth talking of it as seen by him, and therefore, apart from him, should rest contented with identifying this *ego* with its (temperory tenement) *deha*?

24. The *ego* i. e. the substratum of the ego—the (subjective *atman*) is the Universal *Atman*, *Brahma*, being, with it, unique and one, ever-existent and self-illumined, free from all conditions, and by nature all existence, conscious intelligence and joy. The *deha* surely can never be the substratum of this ego: the deha which, is non-existence itself. This is called

---

* It may be argued that if the light of the Atman is unlike that of fire etc for reason of the latter being impotent to dispel all darkness, where did any one observe the absence of darkness, for the light of the universal Atman being present everywhere? The Vedantin will retort, it is only on account of the illumination proceeding from the Atman that darkness or fire or any such thing becomes comprehensible. It is that self-sustaining light which illumines all and is not opposed in its nature to any thing.

real knowledge by the wise (who have realised the real *Atma-tatva.*)

25. The *ego* is free from all change, without any form, un-describable and undecaying or indestructible. The *Deha* &c.

26. The ego is beyond all disease, not within the reach of comprehension, free from all imagination, and all pervading. The Deha &c.

27. It is unaffected by the three *Gunas*—qualities—of matter,—*Sattva*, *Rajas* and *Tamas*—motionless, eternal, ever free from all conditions, undecaying and unique. The *deha* &c.

28. It is, again, free from every impurity—ignorance caused by *Avidya*—Immovable, Infinite, Holy, Immortal, and Unborn. The *deha* &c.

29. Oh you Infinitet fool! when you have got in your own body the holy—in.*an*, which is evidently different from the body, and which is known as the *Purush* (residing in the body of men, in the form of the *ego*), how can you (in spite of this testimony) assert is at this Atman is *nothing*, is mere void,—mere nil?

30. (If abandoning your hypothesis as incompatible with the phenomena even of your own consciousness and existence, you should assert that there may be something, which however cannot be any thing other than the body itself) Oh ignarant one! know the ego within you to he that *Purusha* which is implied in the *Shrutis*, and demonstrated by Reasoning*. It is other than the body in as much as it is the only one of whom you can predicate existence in the real sense of the word: but it is very difficult to be realised as such by people of your cast of mind.

31. The *Atman*, which is the substratum of the *ego* in man, is one: and therefore different from the physical bodies which on the other hand are many. How can this body then be the *Atman*?

---

* Such as: if the body were the ego: the doer and the instrument of any the same action would be the same: which is absurd ∴ the body is not the soul.

32. The ego is well-established as the subject of all perception, whereas the body is the object: this is proved from the fact of our every time saying of the physical body as being "mine" "belonging to me" &c. How can this body &c.

33. It is well-known to us in our daily experience that the *ego* is free from all change (caused by happiness, misery or time. The *ego remains the same* in childhood, young age, old age, though the body changes) whereas the physical body is subject to many. How can &c.

34. The characterstics, oh lord of the ignorant! of this Atman are laid down in the *Sruti* यस्मात्परम् &c. (that is the *Purush* than whom there is nothing higher &c). How can &c.

35. Again the *Shruti* in the Purush Sukta (the hymn to *Purush*) says, all this is *Purush* etc. How then can &c.

36. Even in the *Brihadaranydka* it i[illegible] "this *Purush* is free from every thing etc"; How cou[illegible] [illegible]is body besmeared with endless dirt be this *Purush*?

37. In the same *Shruti*, it is said [illegible]e *Purusha* is self-illumined &c. How could this body whi[illegible] is all darkness and illumined by something quite extraneous, be this *Purusha*?

38. Even that part of the Vedas, which inculcates the performance of various religious ceremonies (as contra-distinguished from that part which inculcates the usefulness of knowledge only) describes the *Atman* as different from the *deha*; and as one, eternal, and therefore subsisting to undergo, after the distruction of its material coil, the results of actions done during any previous life.

39. Even the *astral body* is made up of many things (not one), is unstable, is the object of perception, is subject to change, limited, and non-existent. How could this astral body ever be the *Purusha*?

40. Thus the *Atman* is evidently different from these two bodies, and is the Purusha, the Lord, the Soul of All, every thing in itself, free from all conditions, present in every one as the substratum of the ego, and indestructible.

41. Thus the enunciation of the difference between the two bodies and the *Atman* involving an (indirect) assertion of the reality of the material transitional Universe, given in a manner after the principles of the *Tarkashastra* (Nyaya), compasses but a very insignificant aim in life.*

42. The object however of this enunciation of the vital fundamental difference between the two bodies and the Atman is (not to establish the reality of the material universe but), to dissipate the ignorance of confounding or identifying the Atman with the *dehas.* It yet remains however to clearly demonstrate the unreality of the difference between the two, i. e. it remains clearly to establish that the *dehas* have no existence independent of, and without the *Atman*.

43. As *Chaitanya* or absolute consciousness is but uniform and unique, it cannot admit of a second, it cannot admit of a division. Even the individual soul must then be accepted to be futile, like the delusion of snake in a rope.

44. As through ignorance the rope, appears for the time, to be a snake, so does the unconditioned consciousness—*chit*—, (*Brahma*)—appear in the form of thisso-called material universe.

45. The material cause of this transitional universe can be nothing else than *Brahma*; it follows therefore that the whole universe is Brahma itself and nothing else.

46. In as much as it is ordained that "All is *Atman*," the distinction between the pervading and the pervaded or subject and object, is illusory. This, the highest truth being realised, there could be little room for the distinction of subject and object etc.

47. When the *Shruti* has by denouncing in loud terms the existence of any variety in this (Brahma), fused all the material instrumental and final causes into one unique consciousness, how could there be even the least shadow of any other thing? (as the pervading and pervaded, subject and object etc.)

---

* For it leaves the state of final absolution open to some objections as to its utility or quality, based on the *duality* of the cosmic principle.

48. The *Shruti* has not rested here, but has fastened an awful sin to the belief in the existence of the cause as separate from the effect, in the words "He who led away by *Máyá* or illusion, accepts any variety in this (Absolute *Atman*) passes from death to death (i. e. is born and reborn often and often, and does not attain to final beatitude.)"

49. In as much as the universe exists in the Absolute *Atman*, all-embraciug Brahma, it must be understood to be one with Brahma, its original cause.

50. Moreover the *Shruti* plainly declares that all kinds of names, forms, and actions are sustained in, and through *Brahma*.

51. As the being golden of that which is made of gold is eternal and unchanging, so should be the being *Brahma* of that which proceeds from Brahma.

52. The opinions of that ignorant man, who abides by even the faintest distinction between *Jíva* and *Paramatman*, are very dangerous and pernicious.

53. Distinctions crop up only so long as *duality* is maintained through ignorance, but when the whole is seen as in and of *Atman*, there could not exist the least shadow of distinction.

54. In the condition in which the enlightened identify the whole with *Atman*, there enters not the faintest tinge of delusion, or sorrow, in consequence of the cause of such delusion or sorrow being destroyed with the dissipation of the idea of duality.

55. The Shruti in the Brahadàranyaka has declared that this soul is Brahma, and stands as the soul and substance of the universe.

56. The universe though it be the subject of daily experience, and though it be the object of our constant intercourse (and therefore the living cause of constant delusion, so on &c. vide 54) is unreal like a dream in as much as its *existence* even in the moment next its birth is not provable.

57. For example : dreams are unreal during waking ; nor is the waking condition possible in dreams. Both however are

not to be found in deep absorption, as in dreamless sleep, which again is not experienced in either.

58. Thus, all these three conditions are unreal, being the illusive creations of *maya* with its three *gunas* ; the real, permanent, and unique one is the spirit, which stands aloof from these three *gunas* as the witness of all these conditions.

59. Just as after mature contemplation one does not find a jar in the clay of which it is made, or silver in a lump of nacre, so will the enlightened, on deep meditation, be free from the delusion of believing *Jiva* to be seperate from *Brahma.*

60. The jar exists in earth, the ring in gold, and silver in nacre—but all in *mere name,* so does *Jiva* exist in Brahma.

61. Jut as blueness appears in the sky, or water in the mirage, or as a man is seen in a post, so does the universe appear in the *Atman.*

62. Just as one sees a giant in vacancy ; a castle in the air, or two moons instead of one in the sky, so do ignorant persons see the universe as apart from Brahma.

63. Just as all that appears is water whether in the form of waves or ripples on the surface, or as all again that appears is copper whether as pots or anything, so are all the various forms in the universe but mere manifestations of the *Atman.*

64. Just as it is earth alone that appears under the *name* of a jar, or just as they are the threads only that appear under the *name* of a cloth, so does the Illumined—spirit—go under the *name* of the universe : this spirit can be grasped by the negation of the various imaginary adjuncts superinduced, as *name, form* &c.

65. All intercourse proceeds of, and through *Brahma.* It is through ignorance only that people do not clearly understand that all the jars and pots that appear are but earth and earth alone.

66. Just as the relation of cause and effect between clay and a jar, is constant, so in the question at issue is that of Brahma and the unreal universe; this is loudly declared by Revelation and clearly verified by reason.

67. Just as the consciousness of clay is forced upon our mind, when we are contemplating of a jar only, so even though dealing with the unreal universe, we are through it and in it, rendered forcibly and as it were intuitively conscious of the all pervading Brahma.

68. The *Atman* though ever pure, ever appears impure; just as the same cord appears as a serpent and as a cord to an ignorant and a knowing man respectively.

69. Just as the jar is all earth, so this body is all spirit; the division of *Atman* and *not Atman* is made by the ignorant for no purpose whatever.

70. Just as a cord is understood to be a snake, or a lump of nacre to be a lump of silver, so do the ignorant determine the physical body to be the *Atman*.

71. Just as clay is confounded with the jar made of it, or the threads with the cloth, so do &c.

73. Just as gold is confounded with the rings made of it, or water with the waves surging over it, so &c.

73. Just as a post is taken for a man or the mirage for real water, so do &c.

74. Just as the materials are confounded with the house, or the iron with the sword made of it, so do &c.

75. Just as one seeing at a tree through water sees it inverted, so does the material body appear as Atman to one viewing it through ignorance.

76. Just as to one sailing in a boat every thing appears to be in motion, so &c.

77. Just as a "jaundiced eye sees every thing yellow," so &c.

78. With eyes which are as it were by nature in delusion, every thing appears illusion, so &c.

79. Just as the circle made by a fire-brand, appears like the disc of the sun, so &c.

80. Just as things which are prodigiously large appear small in consequence of distance, so &c.

81. Just as the smallest objects appear very large when viewed through powerful spectacles, so &c.

82. As a floor of glass should be imagined to be filled with water or vice versa, so &c.

83. As one should confound fire with a jewel or vice versa, so &c.

84. As the moon appears to be in motion through the clouds which really are moving, so &c.

85. As some one through confusion loses all distinction between the different points of the compass, so &c.

86. Just as the moon (on account of its reflection) appears moving under the surface of water to some one, so &c.

87. In this manner then, arises the delusion of *matter* (*deha*) in the (spiritual) *Atman*, which (delusion) melts away in the proper realisation of Brahma, by the help of right knowledge.

88. When the whole universe, movable as well as immovable, is known to be Atman by the negation of all substance which appear to exist apart from it, there hardly remains any room even to say that this material body is *Atman.*

89. Oh enlightened one! spend all your time in ever contemplating upon the *Atman*, consuming out, without repining or pain, the fruits of your *Prárabdha.*

90. We now proceed to explain the opinion often declared by the *Shastras* that no body is free from the operations of the law of *Prarabdha*, even though he should have acquired full knowledge of the *Atman.*

91. After the knowledge of the *real* has arisen, there remains no room for *Prarabdha*, in as much as this material body &c. (the plane on which the effects of *Prárabdha* manifest themselves) are then reduced as it were to nothing: just as there is no room for dream after waking.

92. That *Karma* acquired in a previous birth which is called *Prarabdha* (with respect to the present life), has no existence (in the form of *Sanchita* for a future birth) in as much as the man has no other birth to go through.

93. Just as the body at work during dream is a mere illusion, so also is this our physical body. How, then, could an illusion be said to take birth, and when it does not take birth, how again could it be said to exist?

94. The *Vedantas* declare *ignorance* (and *Brahma*) to be the material cause of the universe, just as earth of a jar &c. When this ignorance is destroyed where could the universe subsist?

95. Just as some one should out of confusion understand a rope to be a serpent, so an ignorant man leaving aside the truth sets up this (material) transitory universe in its place.

96. The cord being fully known the serpent disappears at once: so the great substance and support of the universe being known, the universe reduces itself to nothing.

97. As this physical body is thus a mere illusion where could there be any room for the play of *Prarabdha*. Hence the *Prárabdha* &c described in the *Srutis* are for the enlightenment of the ignorant only.

98. The *Plural* used in the Shruti "the highest good of all being reached, all his *Karmas* are destroyed &c." is to negative distinctly the possibility of the action of *Prárabha* (as well as the other two: *Sanchita* and *Kriyamana*).

99. If the ignorant should still maintain the possibility of *Prarabdha* and its action, they will over and above involving themselves in two glaring absurdities, (1. impossibility of *moksha* on account of there being a second—a *Prarabdha*—Superior even to *Brahma*: 2. *moksha* being thus rendered impossible the utility of the *Dnyanmarga*—the way of knowledge—will be nullified), run counter to the teachings of the *Vedanta*. It therefore follows that we must go by the said *Shruti* (Vide Stanza 98) which directs the way to real knowledge.

100. Hence forward (for the instruction of those who require to be taken step by step to the realisation of the said truth) we begin to propound the 15 stages necessary for the acquisition of the knowledge described before. Knowing all these one must use all of them towards acquiring a habit of constant, firm and active meditation.

101. The ever—existent, and all—conscious *Atman* is not realised without a constant and rigid practice (of the rules to be described); therefore one desirous of obtaining absolution must ever meditate upon *Brahma*.

102. 103. The fifteen stages in order are: 1 *Yama*, 2 *Niyama*, 3 *Tyága*, 4 *Mouna*, 5 *Desha*, 6 *Kála*, 7 *Asana*, 8 *Mulabandha*, 9 *Dehasámya*, 10 *Drikshthiti*, 11 *Pranasamyamana*, 12 *Pratyáhára*, 13 *Dháraná*, 14 *Atmadhyána*, 15 *Samádhi*.

104. The natural restraint over all the senses arising from the conviction of *everything* being *Brahma*, is the real *yama*, and it should be repeatedly studied.*

105. The union with the homogeneous (i. e., constant and invariably inseparable consciousness of unity with Brahma), and separation from the heterogenous (such notions as of the universe and Brahma being apart from each other &c.), is the *Niyama* described in the *Shrutis*;—*niyama* the highest happiness; such are thought of by the wise.†

106. The abandonment of this illusion (of form and name) by the recognition of the non-material, ever enlightened Brahma everywhere, is the *Tyága* honoured by the great, as leading to immediate absolution.‡

---

* अहिंसा, सत्य, मस्तेयं, ब्रह्मचर्यं, क्षमा, धृतिः । दया, अैवं, मिताहारः, शौचं, चैवयमादश ॥ १६–१–॥ हठप्रदीपिका ॥ The *yama* of *Hatha* or physical, *yoga*, comprises ten formulas of conduct all however tending to secure the mental condition described in 104. The same remark holds good for all other illustrations to be cited from works on *Hatha yoga*.

† तपः, संतोष, मास्तिक्यं, दान, मीश्वरपूजनं,। सिद्धांतवाक्यश्रवणं, न्हीमीति, श्च तपो, हुतम् ॥ नियमादशसंप्रोक्तायोगशास्त्रविशारदैः ॥ idem.

‡ This *Tyága* must it seems be understood as opposed to the *Tyaga* or abandonment of one's duties and *Karmas* in life—as understood by superficial *Vedantins*.

107. The enlightened must ever try to possess that *Mouna*—that indescribable Brahma—which, though the mind turns back baffled from it, and though words cannot describe it, is ever to be found in those who are devoted to the path of pure knowledge.*

108.-109. Who can describe that (Brahma) which words are not able to comprehend? If this universe of illusion even were subjected to examination, that also is beyond the reach of speech. Hence this may be the real *Mauna* (viz. abandonment of all doubts as to the relation of *Brahma* and *Jagat*) known to the wise as *Sahaja Sthiti*—Native condition;—whereas the *Mouna* ordinarily known in the form of restraining the tongue is pronounced by the Adwaitee, to be simply childish.

110. That is the real "solitary, *Desha*" (place) wherein the universe does not exist in the beginning, middle, or end; and which is to be found through the whole of this (material life.)†

111. In consequence of its being the support and sustenance of all actions, such as even the winking of the eye &c, of all up to Brahmà and others, the word *Kala* indicates the real uninterrupted and unique fountain of joy. (*Brahma*).‡

112. That in which one can easily and uninterruptedly meditate upon *Brahma* is the most proper *Asan*, and not any other interfering with one's ease and happiness.§

113. That which is the eternal and well-known container of

---

* This *mouna* is opposed to the ordinary practice of restraining the tongue &c.

† सुराज्ये धार्मिके देशे सुभिक्षे निरुपद्रवे । धनुःप्रमाणपर्यंते शिलाग्निजलवर्जिते । एकांते मठिकामध्ये स्थातव्यं हठयोगिना ॥ हठ. प्र८॥

‡ This kála may be taken as opposed to the time observed in performing pranayama &c.

§ As opposed to the 8 or any indefinite number of *Asans* as *Siddhasan Padmasan*, *Mayurasan* &c.—all implying certain positions of the body accompanied by an amount of physical exertion and exercise.

the universe of being, and that in which the *Siddhas* are ever sitting at ease, is the real *Siddhásana.**

114. That which is the origin of all Being, and that on whom depends the original (ignorance) obstruction of the *manas*, is the *mulabandha* to be always practiced, and is the only one to be taken up by student's of *Raj* or mental *yoga.*†

115. That is *Dehasámya* by which the physical body (naturally crooked and distorted) becomes on account of its being viewed as of Brahma, immersed in Brahma. If this is not accomplished, the forcible straightening of the limbs, like that of the dead trunk of a tree, is certainly the least of *Dehasámya.*

116. That one, having converted his internal eye into one of pure knowledge, should view the whole of this transitional universe as Brahma, is the real concentration of the eye *(Driksthiti)*; and not the one wherein the eye is fixed on the tip of one's nose.‡

117. Or, the fixing of the (internal) ego on that in which the triad of the seer, sight and seen is reduced to unity—is the real concentration &c.

118. The constant and permanent obstruction of all the senses (internal), through the process of viewing upon all objects such as the mind and its creations &c. as in and of Brahma is called *Pránáyáma.*§

---

* मेंढ्रादुपरि विन्यस्य सव्यंगुल्फंतथोपरि । गुल्फांतरं चनिक्षिप्य सिध्धासनमिदं भवेत् ॥ हठ. प्र० ॥.

† पार्ष्णिभागेनसंपिड्ययोनिमाकुंचयेदगुदम् । अपानमूर्ध्वमाकृष्यमूलबंधोऽभिधीयते ॥ हठ. प्र० ॥.

‡ Compare the various *Mudrás* of *Hatha yoga.*

§ चलेवातेचलंचित्तं निश्चलेनिश्चलंभवेत् ।
योगीस्थाणुत्वमाप्नोतिततोवायुंनिरोधयेत्
* * * * *
बध्धपद्मासनोयोगीप्राणंचंद्रेणपूरयेत् ।
धारयित्वायथाशक्ति भूयःसूर्येणरेचयेत् ॥
प्राणंसूर्येणचाकृष्यपूरयेदुदरंशनैः ।
विधिवत्कुंभकंकृत्वापुनश्चंद्रेणरेचयेत् ॥ हठ० प्र० ॥

119, 120. The negation (as by resolving into Brahma &c.) of this phenomenal illusion, is the real *Rechaka* (blowing out of the breath retained in the lungs); and the conviction "I am Brahma" is the real *Puraka* (the drawing in of the breath); and then the immovable concentration on that very conviction is the real *kumbhaka* (the retention of the breath in the lungs for some time). This is the real course of *Práṇáyáma* * but to be followed by the enlightened, whereas, the ignorant will go on torturing their nose for nothing.

121. The absorption of the mind in the ever-enlightened *Brahma* by resolving all objects into *Atman*, should be known as *Pratyáhára*, and should be practised by those who are desirous of absolution.†

122. The steadiness of the mind arising from the recognition of *Brahma*, wherever it travels or goes, is the real and great *Dháraná*.‡

123. The independent (free from any other idea as of *matter*, &c.) existence consequent upon the full sense of Being; arising from the conviction "I am *Brahma*," is the condition conducive to the highest joy, and is described as *Dhyána*.§

It will be observed that the difference in the practice here indicated constitutes the real point of difference between Hatha or physical and Raja or mental yoga. The point to be reached by either is the same—restraint over the mind and its creations, and attainment of the condition of eternal *Samádhi* or concentration or identification with the principle of the universe—but the ways leading to this end are different. The former holds that the mind will be naturally and easily controlled by shutting up all the avenues of its communication with the external world—viz. the breath &c. The latter holds and perhaps correctly holds—that the shortness or length of the breath, is but an indication of the State of the mind and that therefore instead of fruitlessly and unnaturally stifling this breath we had much better curb the cause of all this breath and everything viz. the giant मनस् or the mind.

* The order of the process indicated in the Hatha yoga is 1st *Puraka*, then *Kumbhaka* and then *Rechaka*.

† स्वविषयासंप्रयोगेचित्तस्यस्वरूपानुकारइन्द्रियाणां प्रत्याहारः ॥ पात॰ यो॰ सू॰ ॥ २. ५३. ॥ ‡ देशबन्धश्चित्तस्यधारणा ॥ पात॰ यो॰ सू॰ ॥३.१.॥.

§ तत्रप्रत्ययैकतानताध्यानम् ॥ पा॰ यो॰ सू॰ ॥ ३. २. ॥

124. The negation of all mental action, by the mind's being reduced to a state beyond all change, and by its being ever merged into Brahma is called conscious *Samádhi.**

125. This natural course of joy should be studied by the wise only so long as they acquire the power of, at the spur of the moment, collecting and concentrating themselves.

126. Then he (the practitioner) being free from the necessity of going through the said and similar processes, becomes the best of all accomplished successful ascetics. The condition of such an ascetic cannot easily be described in words or conceived by the mind.

127. 128. Even while assiduously practising *Samádhi,* numerous difficulties crop up in the way: Such as being put off the point of concentration; idleness; desire of illusive enjoyments; sleep; paralysis of the intellect; being drawn off by temporary objects of the universe; egoistical immersion in transitory joy; and dullness or torpidity of the mind. One knowing Brahma should try to gradually evade all these one after another.†

129. If one concentrates his mind on some object, or even on void, he becomes entirely filled with that object or that void: so one who fixes his mind on *Brahma* becomes completely

---

* Even in *Raj yoga* समाधि is sometimes concisely defined as समाधिः संविदुत्पत्तिः॥. also as तदेवार्थमात्रनिर्भासं स्वरूपशून्यमिव समाधिः॥ पा० यो० सू० ॥ ३. ३. The Hatha yoga has यदासंक्षीयतेप्राणोमानसंचप्रलीयते । तदासमरसत्वंच-समाधि रभिधीयते ॥ हठ० प्र० ॥

† एवमस्याङ्गिनो निर्विकल्पस्य लयविक्षेपकषायरसास्वादलक्षणाश्चत्वारोविघ्नाः संभवंति । लयस्तावदखंडवस्त्वनवलंबनेन चित्तवृत्तेर्निद्रा । अखंडवस्त्वनवलंबनेन चित्तवृत्तेरन्यावलंबनं विक्षेपः । लयविक्षेपाभावेऽपिचित्तवृत्तेरागादिवासनयास्तब्धीभावादखंडवस्त्वनवलंबनंकषायः । अखंडवस्त्वनवलंबनेनाऽपिचित्तवृत्तेः सविकल्पकानंदास्वादनंरसास्वादः । समाध्यारंभसमयेसविकल्पकानंदास्वादनंवा। अनेनविघ्नचतुष्टयेन विरहितंचित्तंनिर्वातदीपवदचलं सदखंडचैतन्यमात्रमवतिष्ठते यदातदानिर्विकल्पकसमाधिरुच्यते ॥ वेदान्तसार ॥.

full of *Brahma*, sees *Brahma* everywhere. One should therefore study to become perfect i.-e. full of *Brahma.*

130. Those persons who abandon this holy and sublime mental attitude of *Brahma*, live to no purpose, and are though men equal to brutes.

131. Hail to those, happy and virtuous beings who, on the other hand, know this state and knowing it grow perfect in it by constant practice. Respect is due to them at the hands of all the three worlds.

132. Those who have reached to the perfection of this state of *Brahma*, and have thoroughly mastered it, the ever-existent, are *Brahma* itself; and not those who merely talk glibly about the matter.

133. Those again who are clever at talking about *Brahma*, but are void of any real attempt towards reaching to that state and are fast bound to the ties of transitory pleasures,—have to pass and repass (in various births), in consequence of this their hypocracy and ignorance.

134. (The enlightened) never remain even for a minuute, without uniting their souls with *Brahma*: as did Brahma, Sanakadika, Shuka and other *Mahatmas*.

135. The cause is reflected in the effect but not the effect in the cause. Hence well-directed thought will prove that on account of the relative non-existence of the effect in the cause the cause itself also could hardly be called the cause of that effect; i.e. must vanish as the active instrumental cause of anything—but should ever stand by itself—all existence, all intelligence and all joy.

136. Thus there will remain that effulgent universal essence, which transcends both mind and speech. This should repeatedly be studied from such ordinary illustrations as of earth and the jar made of it &c.

137. Perseverance in this direction brings about, in those whose minds are sufficiently enlightened, the state of constant

knowledge which ultimately leads to its spontaneous and natural unification with *Brahma.*

138. Every student should first contemplate and grasp the cause as existing apart from its effect; he would then constantly see by inseparable relation the cause in the effect.

139. Thus having contemplated the cause as reflected in the effect, the effect must be entirely dismissed (from the mind). When this is done, the cause will cease to be such, and what will remain will be the ever existent, ever conscious, all pervading indescribable *Brahma.*

140. A man becomes that on which he resolutely and persistently thinks. This we infer from the ordinary illustration of the bee and the worm.*

141. All this universe visible or invisible, (implying the triad of the seer, seen and sight) is one eternal consciousness.

142. The enlightened should always look upon the universe as one in and of Brahma, by resolving the visible into the invisible;—thus will he, through his mind being ever filled with the bliss of identifying himself with this universal consciousness, easily attain to the condition of eternal happiness.

143. This with the parts set forth above is *Ráj* or mental *yoga* mixed with *Hatha* or physical *Yoga* prescribed for those who have already lost great portion of their taste for the pleasures of the senses.

144. To those whose mind is completely ripe (by विवेक, वैराग्य &c.) this (Ráj Yoga) alone (without any *Hatha* or physical yoga) is useful;-this *yoga* again being one easily accessible even to those who are devoted to their teachers, or to their favourite gods, &c.

---

* The bee takes hold of any small worm and even while it is alive puts it into a small hole of clay specially prepared, and blocks up the opening. The worm thinking in its dark prison of the bee and bee alone, remains there till the bee returning at its proper time, removes the clay and with a sting awakens the worm which immediately flies out another bee incarnate.

APPENDIX.

॥ शुध्धपत्रम् ॥

अशुध्धम्	शुध्धम्	पृष्ठे	पङ्क्तौ
०संदेहो.....ध्धा.	०संदेहो.....ध्धे	३	९
द्दष्टरि.....द्दष्टृता.	द्रष्टरि.....द्रष्टृता.	९	६
मप्यप्रामाणिकत्व.	०प्रमाणत्व.	,,	१३
आवृत्ति.	आवृति.	११, १९, २६, २७, २८, २९,	१३, ३-९-७-१०-११, २१, १, २१-२३, ४.
गछतीति.	गच्छतीति.	१२	१०
दशायाप्रभा०	०यामभा०	१४	२
आवृत्तौ.	आवृतौ.	,,	७
आवृत्ता.	आवृता.	,,	११
०न्यात्वगातित्वेन	०गतत्वेन.	,,	,,
स्तिश्टति.	स्तिष्ठति.	,,	२३
दश्य.	दृश्य.	१७	८
ध्यायेदश्या०.	०दृश्या०	,,	१२
तेष.	तेषां.	,,	१४
वेशाद०.	०शाद्द०.	१८	१२
यस्तध्धी०.	यःस्त०	२१	९
पड्विधः	०धाः	,,	१८
पाड्विधासमा०.	०धाःस०	२२	७
भोगोदव.	भोगादेव.	२३	२०
०वांचीच्छन्ना०.	०वच्छि०.	२४	२२
चिद्यावछिन्नो.....रावछि०	०च्छि०.....च्छि०	२५	१०
अनयोर्जा०	०र्जी०	२७	२१
तऐते.	तएते.	२८	२

तांगछत्ये०.	तांगच्छत्ये.	,,	६
मापद्यते.	मापद्यंते.	,,	६
अशुध्दम्	शुध्दम्	पृष्ठे	पङ्क्तौ
स्तगंछांति.	०गच्छांति.	,,	८
०तं ॥	तम् ॥	,,	१८
*दृढयतुं.	द्रढयितुं.	२९	२२
प्रतिभासिकं.	प्रातिभासिकम्.	२९	२४
प्रातिभासीका०.	प्रातिभासिका०.	३०	१
जलस्थोपरि.	०स्योप०.	३१	१६
धिष्ठानानान०.	०ष्टानान०	,,	२१
तद्वारेण.	तद्द्वारेण.	,,	२४
सेक.	सिक.	३२	८
०त्वनीरज....त्वनी...नारि...नरि०॥ त्वान्नी..त्वान्नी..नीर..नीर०		,,	२१
द्वयात्मकानिद्रा.	०त्मकनिद्रा.	३३	१२
०वच्छिनस्य.	०वच्छिन्नस्य.	,,	१९
प्रतिष्ठेव.	प्रविष्टइव.	,,	२३
मवाच्छिनत्वं.	मवच्छिन्नत्वं.	३४	१०

---

* ग्रंथे स्थानान्तरेऽपि दृढयतीत्यादिकस्य स्थाने द्रढयतीत्यादिकं यथायोग्यं शिष्टैरुह्यम्.

॥गुरुस्तुतिः॥

किंवाणूनभिवादयेऽथ पुरुषं किं सप्रधानं भज
आत्मानन्दविलीनचित्तरचितोपाधौ समाधौ शये ।
प्राधीये श्रुतिमेव वेति विविधैस्तर्कैर्मुधा ताम्यताम्
सर्वेषामपि मोदमात्रविभवस्त्वेकः शरण्यो भवान् ॥ १ ॥
कान्ताश्लेषविशेषवीतवयसां याःप्रेममिष्टा मुदो
यावा पुत्रकलत्रधान्यकवलासक्तात्मनां प्रीतयः ।
यास्तत्त्वार्थविचारपेशलधियां शास्त्रे स्वकर्मण्यपि
ज्ञानोद्रेकविलीनमोहकलिले ताः पर्यवस्यन्ति नः ॥ २ ॥
मोहान्धकारकमलाहतजीवजन्तु
र्ज्ञाताकथं स्वकमले विमलैकभावम् ।
त्वत्पादपांशुघृणिभीरविभावभाग्भिः
पूज्यैर्विनाप्रविततैःशुचिभिःप्रशान्तैः ॥ ३ ॥
देहिज्ञानमिति प्रकामविरसं कर्त्तव्यतारूपिणे
प्राप्स्ये तत् स्वयमेववेति विकलं दीनत्वहीनंवचः ।
स्तुत्यर्थोऽपि कथं विधास्यति फलं त्वद्भावमन्दार्थधीः
सर्वज्ञप्रतिबोधनाय वितता वाणी विमूढायते ॥ ४ ॥
पुण्यश्रेणिप्रचयवितातिन्यस्तलीलावधाने
दुष्टाचारप्रगुणिततमोनोदखेलप्रखिन्ने ।
भक्तानां वा भवजलतरीभावमाप्ते प्रशान्ते
ध्यानच्छेदे प्रणयनतय श्चिन्तनीया विभो नः ॥ ५ ॥

(नवीनम्)

ॐ

दृग्दृश्यविवेकइत्यपरपर्यायः

श्रीवाक्यसुधाग्रन्थः

॥ प्रारभ्यते ॥

॥ श्रीगणेशायनमः ॥ ॐनमोभगवतेवासुदेवाय ॥ यस्मात्सर्वं
समुत्पन्नंचराचरमिदंजगत् ॥ इदंनमोनटेशायतस्मैकारुण्यरूपिणे ॥ १ ॥
कारणंखादिजगतामरणार्थं मनागसम् ॥ वारणाननमात्मानमद्वयंसमुपास्म
हे ॥२॥ परापश्यंत्यादिदेहांपणताभीष्टदायिनीम् ॥ सत्यज्ञानानंदरूपा
ध्यायेह्याद्यांसरस्वतीम्॥ ३ ॥नत्वाश्रीभारतीतीर्थविद्यारण्यमुनीश्वरौ ॥ मयावा
क्यसुधाटीकायथामतिविरच्यते॥ ४॥ नख्यातिर्लाभपूजेचटीकाकरणकारणम्
नविद्वत्तावलंकात्रमुक्तिरेवात्रकारणम् ॥५॥ प्रारिप्सितस्यग्रंथस्याविघ्नेनपरि
समाप्तिप्रचयगमनाय शिष्टाचारपरिपालनायचकेवलकूटस्थप्रत्यग्बोधरूपपर
मात्मस्वरूपानुस्मरणलक्षणंमंगलमाचरन्सच्चिदानंदाखंडैकरसस्वरूपाऽवस्था
नलक्षणस्यमोक्षस्यतत्त्वमस्यादिमहावाक्यार्थापरोक्षज्ञानफलकत्वात् ।वाक्यार्थ
ज्ञानस्यचान्वयव्यतिरेकाभ्यांपदार्थपरिशोधनपूर्वकत्वात् । पदार्थपरिशो
धनस्यप्रसिद्धानुवादेनाप्रसिद्धं निरूपणीयमितिन्यायेनप्रतिशरीरमहमहमिति
प्रसिद्धजीववाचकत्वंपदार्थपरिशोधनपूर्वकत्वात् । श्रीमच्छारीरकमहाशा
स्त्रेश्रीमद्भाष्यकारैः प्रतिपादितमर्थंहृदिनिधायप्राण्यनुजिघृक्षयादृग्दृश्यावि
वेकद्वाराप्राधान्येनत्वंपदार्थपरिशोधनपरमिदंप्रकरणमारभमाणः परमकृपा
निधिः श्रीभारतीतीर्थगुरुः प्रकरणप्रतिपाद्यमानमर्थंसंक्षिप्यप्रथमश्लोकेनता
न्दर्शयति रूपमिति ॥

रूपंदृश्यंलोचनंदृग्दृग्दृश्यंदृक्तुमानसम् ॥
दृश्याधीवृत्तयःसाक्षीदृगेवनतुदृश्यते ॥१॥

लोकेचक्षुरिंद्रियग्राह्यंयद्रूपमस्तितत्सर्वंदृश्यंभवति । तद्ग्राहकंचक्षुरिंद्रियंस्वग्राह्यापेक्षयादृग्भवति । तथा । तत्पुनश्चक्षुरिंद्रियंस्वस्मादभ्यांतरस्य मनसोदृश्यंभवति । स्वभास्यचक्षुरिंद्रियापेक्षयामानसमपिदृग्भवति । मनसःसर्वेंद्रियावभासकत्वसामर्थ्यंद्योतयतितुशब्दः । धीवृत्तयःअंतःकरणस्यवक्ष्यमाणवृत्तयस्तदविद्याकार्यत्वेनजडरूपत्वात्दृश्याभवंति ॥ साक्षीशरीरत्रयविलक्षणः प्रत्यगात्मादृगेवभवतिद्रष्टैवभवति ॥ एवकारेणार्थाद्दृश्यत्वेनिषिद्धेपिकंठतोपिदृश्यत्वंनिषेधयन्प्रत्यगात्मनोद्रष्टृत्वमेवदृढयति नतुदृश्यत इति ॥ साक्षिणिवर्त्तमानस्यदृक्कस्यसर्वांतरत्वेसापेक्षितत्वाभावात्ततस्तस्य लोचनमानसयोर्वर्त्तमानदृक्कवैलक्षण्यंद्योतयतिद्वितीयस्तुशब्दः ॥ साक्षिणः दृश्यत्वमप्रामाणिकमिति यस्मात्तस्मात्कालत्रयेपिदृक्कमेवास्यस्वरूपमितिभावः ॥१॥ एवंप्रकरणप्रतिपाद्यमानमर्थंसंक्षिप्यप्रथमश्लोकेनदर्शयित्वेदानींप्रथमश्लोकस्यप्रथमपादेनदर्शितमर्थंद्वितीयश्लोकेनदर्शयति नीलपीतेति ॥

नीलपीतस्थूलसूक्ष्मह्रस्वदीर्घादिभेदतः ॥
नानाविधानिरूपाणिपश्येल्लोचनमेकधा ॥ २ ॥

दृश्यत्वदृक्कयोर्नानात्वैकत्वहेतुकत्वान्नीलपीताद्यनेकभेदभिन्नत्वेनदृश्यत्वं प्राप्तानिरूपाणिचक्षुरिंद्रि यंस्वयंस्वग्राह्यरूपभेदानुकूलस्वरूपभेदमगृहीत्वैवैकरूपेणैवपश्येत्गृह्णीयात् अतएवास्यदृक्कंस्यादितिभावः ॥ · ॥ एवंप्रथमश्लोकस्यद्वितीयपादोक्तमर्थं स्पष्टीकुर्वन्चक्षुरिंद्रिये प्रदर्शितंन्यायंश्रोत्रादींद्रियेष्वप्यतिदिशति आंध्यमिति ॥

आंध्यमांद्यपटुत्वेपुनेत्रधर्मेषुचैकधा ॥
संकल्पयेन्मनःश्रोत्रत्वगादौयोज्यतामिदम् ॥३॥

आंध्यंनामसामान्याकारेणापिस्वविषयग्रहणासामर्थ्यं विषयसामान्याकारग्राहकत्वंमांद्यं स्वविषयसूक्ष्मविशेषाकारग्रहणसामर्थ्यंपटुत्वमेव मत्र नेत्रधर्मेष्वांध्यमांद्यादिभेदभिन्नेष्वपिनानात्वेनैहेतुनाभास्यमानान्नेत्रधर्मान्

भास्यभेदानुरूपस्वरूपभेदमगृहित्वैकरूपेणैवमनः संकल्पयेत् । मम चक्षुरंधं ममचक्षुर्मंदंममचक्षुः पट्विति । अतएवास्य मनसोदृश्यकंभवतीत्यर्थः ॥ श्रोत्रत्वगादावित्यत्रचशब्दःसंबध्यते श्रोत्रत्वग्जिव्हाघ्राणेष्वपीदंस्वविषयापेक्षयादृश्यकंस्वभासकमानसापेक्षयादृश्यत्वं यथोचितंबाधियार्दिकंचयोज्यतामुह्यतामित्यर्थः ॥ एकस्मिन्निंद्रियेदृग्दृश्यविवेकंदर्शयित्वाश्रोत्रादींद्रियांतरेष्वप्येवंयोज्यतामित्यतिदिशति ॥ आचार्यस्यस्वशिष्यैःस्वबुद्ध्याक्रियमाणोदृग्दृश्यविवेकएव पुरुषार्थोपायोभवतीत्यभिप्रायः ॥ ३ ॥ प्रथमश्लोकस्योत्तरार्द्धेसाक्षीदृगेवेत्यंतेनग्रंथेनप्रदर्शितमर्थंविशदयति कामइति ॥

कामःसंकल्पसंदेहोश्रध्धाश्रध्धाधृतीतरे ॥
ह्रीर्धीर्भीरित्येवमादीन्भासयत्येकधाचितिः ॥४॥

रज्ज्वज्ञानाद्रज्ज्वारोपिताःसर्पादयोरज्जुरिवस्वाज्ञानात्स्वस्मिन्नारोपिताः कामःसंकल्पोविचिकित्साश्रध्धाधृतिरधृतिर्ह्रीर्धीर्भीरित्येतेसर्वेमनएवेति । बृहदारण्यकश्रुत्युक्तानादिशब्देनसंगृहीतानैतरेयोपनिषदुक्तान्संज्ञादींश्चस्वरूपज्ञानापनोद्यानेतान्सर्वानप्यंतःकरणवृत्तिविशेषान्स्वगतादिभेदरहितसच्चिदानंदलक्षणब्रह्माभिन्नकूटस्थप्रत्यग्रूपासर्वसाक्षिणीचितिरेकधाभासयाति । विकारकारणाभावात्स्वभास्यावस्तुभूतविकारानुरूपं स्वगतविकारमंतरेणाप्येकरूपेणैवप्रकाशयतीतियावत् ॥ ४ ॥ इंद्रियमनसोरुक्तन्यायेनोक्तलक्षणायाश्चितेरपिदृश्यत्वंस्यादित्याशंकायांदृश्यत्वस्यद्रष्टृपूर्वकत्वाच्चितेर्द्रष्टृत्वेन चित्यंतरांगीकारेणानवस्थाख्योदोषःस्यात् ॥ चितेश्चितिरेवद्रष्ट्रीत्यस्मिन्पक्षेपिकर्मकर्तृविरोधःस्यात् ॥ तस्मात्प्रकाशांतरनिरपेक्षतयास्वयंप्रकाशमानायाश्चितेर्दृश्यत्वंनस्यादित्यर्थतोदर्शयन्मुख्यतःस्वव्यतिरिक्तांतःकरणादियुष्मद्धर्म्यश्चितेर्वैलक्षण्यंनतुदृश्यतइत्यंशविवरणेनानेनश्लोकेनदर्शयति नोदेतीति ॥

॥ नोदेतिनास्तमेत्येषानवृद्धिंयातिनक्षयं ॥
॥ स्वयंविभात्यथोन्यानिभासयेत्साधनंविना ॥५॥

यत्साक्षादपरोक्षादपरोक्षाद्ब्रह्मेति श्रुत्युक्तप्रकारेणविद्वदपरोक्षतांचितेरर्थात्सूचयन्नुक्तलक्षणांचितिंपरामृशत्येषेति ॥ सर्वसाक्षिण्येषाचितिरहमादियुष्मदर्थवत्प्रागभावाभावान्नोदेति । नोत्पद्यते ॥ प्रध्वंसाभावाभावान्नास्तमेति । अंतंविनाशंनाप्नोति । वृद्धिक्षयौताभ्यामुपलक्षितौ । अस्तित्वपरिणामौचनप्राप्नोति । सर्वथाप्येकरूपत्वात् ॥ उत्पत्त्यनंतरंभाविव्यावहारिकास्तित्वमेवविकारांतःपातित्वेननिषिध्यते । नतुस्वरूपास्तित्वं । तस्याविकारित्वेननिषेद्धुमशक्यत्वात् ॥ चितेःषड्भावविकाररहितत्वेहेतुंदर्शयति स्वयंविभातीति ॥ एषाचितिःस्वस्यप्रकाशांतरनिरपेक्षतयास्वयंप्रकाशमाना सतीसच्चिदानंदात्मकस्वरूपप्रकाशानंतरमेवस्वव्यतिरिक्तान्यखिलान्यारोपितवस्तुनिभासयेत्प्रकाशयेत् । तमेवभातमनुभातिसर्वंतस्यभासासर्वमिदंविभातीतिश्रुतेः । सविकल्पस्यज्ञानस्यनिर्विकल्पकज्ञानपूर्वकत्वाच्च ॥ अत्रानुमानद्वयंसूचितं । अस्मत्प्रत्ययविषया एषाचितिःषड्भावविकाररहिताप्रकाशांतरनैरपेक्ष्येणस्वयंप्रकाशमानत्वात् । यत्षड्भावविकाररहितंनभवतितत्प्रकाशांतरनैरपेक्ष्येणस्वयंप्रकाशमानमपिनभवति । यथायुष्मत्प्रत्ययविषयोहमादिः ॥ उक्तलक्षणैषाचितिःषड्भावविकाररहिता । प्रकाशांतरनैरपेक्ष्येण स्वव्यतिरिक्तवस्त्ववभासकत्वात् । यन्नैवंतन्नैवं । यथाहमादिरिति ॥ एवमुक्तप्रकारेणस्वयंप्रकाशमानत्वात्षड्भावविकाररहितत्वाच्च युष्मदर्थवैलक्षण्येसमार्थितेसतिचितेः कालत्रयेपिदृक्त्वमेवस्वरूपं नतुदृश्यत्वमित्यर्थात्समर्थितंभवति ॥ अदृष्टंद्रष्टृश्रुतंश्रोत्रमतंमंत्रविज्ञातंविज्ञातृनदृष्टेर्द्रष्टारंपश्येन्नश्रुतेःश्रोतारंशृणुयान्नमतेर्मंतारंमन्वीथाः नविज्ञातेर्विज्ञातारंविजानीयाइत्यादिश्रुतिसहस्रेणाप्ययमेवार्थस्तात्पर्येणप्रतिपाद्यतइति ॥ अतोयुष्मत्प्रत्ययविषयांतःकरणादिरूपंदृश्यमेव । अस्मत्प्रत्ययावलंबनभूतायाःप्रत्यक्चितेःस्वरूपंदृक्त्वमेव। अतःप्रत्यक्चितिरेवपरंब्रह्मेत्ययमेवाभिप्रेतार्थः ॥ १ ॥ ननु युष्मदर्थावभासकत्वंप्रथमश्लोकेसाक्षिणइत्युक्तं । अत्रतुचितेरित्युक्तं । अतःपूर्वापरविरोधइतिचेत्तन्नैषदोषः ॥ प्रथमश्लोकोक्तसाक्षिणए

वात्रचितिशब्देनपरामृष्टत्वात् । तस्यैवपुनःप्रथमश्लोकार्थविवरणेनप्रकरण परिसमाप्तिपर्यंतेनोत्तरंग्रथसंदर्भेणापितत्रतत्रसाक्षिशब्देनपरामृष्टत्वात् । साक्षी । चितिः । चित् । चैतन्यं । ज्ञानं । बोधः । प्रत्यगात्मा । कूटस्थ इत्यादिशब्दानामेकार्थपर्यवसायित्वाच्च ॥ ननुतर्हियुष्मदर्थस्यांतःकरणस्यसापेक्षकंदृक्कमपिनसंभवतिभौतिकत्वेनजडात्मकत्वाद्घटादिवत् । दृष्टरिनास्तिदृश्यत्वंदृश्यस्यदृष्टृतानाहि । दृश्यरूपस्यकुड्यादेर्द्रष्टृतानाहिदृश्यतइतिपुराणवचनाच्च ॥ तथासतितस्यसंसारोनोपपद्यते ॥ अथवापूर्वोक्तप्रकारेणाहमादिविलक्षणस्यकूटस्थस्यस्वयंप्रकाशप्रत्यग्बोधरूपस्यसाक्षिणश्चजाग्रदादिविमोक्षांतःसंसारोनोपपद्यते । तस्यासंगोदासीनत्वात् । योसंसारीनभवतिसोऽसंगोदासीनोपिनभवति । यथाहमादिः । असंगोह्ययंपुरुषःइत्यादिश्रुतिसद्भावात् ॥ एवंउक्तप्रकारेणांतः करणतत्साक्षिणोरूभयोप्यसंसारित्वेसमर्थितेसतिसंसाराभवात्तन्निवर्तकज्ञानस्यापिनै रर्थक्यं स्यात् ॥ ततस्तत् ज्ञानप्रतिपादकवेदांतवाक्यानामप्यप्रामाणिकत्वप्रसंगःस्यात् ॥ पुनरुक्तलक्षणस्याशेषविशेषशून्यस्यसाक्षिणः शब्दप्रवृत्तिनिमित्तषष्ठ्यादिराहितत्वेनवेदांतवाक्यैर्विधिमुखेनप्रतिपाद्यमानत्वासंभवात् अतन्निरसनमात्रेणतद्रूपाप्रसिद्धेश्चशास्त्रस्याप्रामाण्यंप्रसज्येत ॥ एवंपरंपरयानेकदोषसंभवात्साक्षिण : कूटस्थत्वंस्वयंप्रकाशमानत्वादिकमप्यप्रामाणिकंस्यादित्यनेकदोषमाशंक्यांतः करणप्रतिफलितानिर्वचनीयचिच्छायांगीकारेसतिसर्वोपिदोष : परिहृतः स्यादित्यभिप्रेत्यचिच्छायांतावदंगीकरोति चिच्छायेति ॥

चिच्छायावेशतोबुद्धौभानंधीस्तुद्विधास्थिता ॥
एकाहंकृतिरन्यास्यादंतःकरणरूपिणी ॥६॥

चिच्छायावेशतोबुद्धौभानं । रजतसुवर्णादिवद्बहुविधपरिणामार्हमंतःकरणाख्यंद्रव्यमत्रबुधिशब्देनधीशब्देनचोच्यते । तस्यांतःकरणस्यकर्तृस्वरूपवृत्तिमानंशोहंकृतिशब्देनोच्यते ॥ करणस्वरूपोंतः शब्दवाच्याहामिदमात्मक

वृत्त्यंशोंतःकरणशब्देनोच्यते ॥ तत्रश्रोत्रादिकरणापेक्षयांतः करण त्वादंतःकरणं ॥ बुध्यतेऽनयास्वरूपमितिबुद्धिः । तस्यांचिच्छाया वेशत श्चिच्छायाचित्प्रतिबिंबस्तस्यावेशस्ततोभानंस्यात् । स्वभावतो जडरूपाप्यनुप्रविष्टचैतन्यबलाद्बुधिः स्वयंप्रकाशमानेवभवतीतिया वत् ॥ धीस्तुद्विधास्थितातुशब्दोवधारणे।भ्रामकसन्निधौलोहवत्साक्षिसन्निधौ बहुविधचेष्टांकुर्वतीसाधीर्द्विधैवस्थितातयोर्मध्येएकाधी रहंकृतिशब्दवाच्या कर्तृरूपास्यात्। अन्याधीर्मनःशब्दवाच्यांतःकरणरूपिणीस्यात् ॥ कामादी नांसंज्ञादीनांचसर्वेषामप्यंत : करणपरिणामविशेषाणांमनोबुध्यहंकारचित्ता ख्येंतःकरणचतुष्टयेष्वंतर्भूतत्वात् । बुद्धिचित्तयोरपियथाक्रममहंकारमनसोरे वांतर्भूतत्वात् । वृत्तिमद्वृत्तिलक्षणाकारद्वयव्यतिरिक्तांतः करणाकारांतरस्य निरूपितुमशक्यत्वाच्चित्कर्मभूताबुद्धि : स्वविकारानुकारिणानुप्रविष्ट चैतन्येनसहिताहंकारमनः शब्दवाच्यकर्तृकरणात्मकवृत्तिमद्वृत्तिलक्षणाका रद्वयेनैकावस्थितेतिभावः ॥ ६ ॥ उक्तलक्षणयोरहंकारमनसोर्मध्येहंकार स्यचिच्छाययासहतप्तायःपिंडवत्तादात्म्यात्तेनसच्चिदाभासाहंकारेणतादात्म्या ज्जडरूपोपिदेहश्चेतनत्वंप्राप्नुयादित्याह छायेति ॥

छायाहंकारयोरैक्यंतप्तायः पिंडवन्मतं ॥
तदहंकारतादात्म्याद्देहश्चेतनतामगात् ॥ ७ ॥

छायाहंकारयोरैक्यंतप्तायःपिंडवद्वह्निसंबंधेनतद्रूपंतप्तायःपिंडवन्मतम भिप्रेतंयथादृष्टांते प्ययमग्नि रिदमय इतिपृथक्करणमशक्यं तथादार्ष्टांति के प्ययमहंकार इयंचिच्छायाइत्यहंकारस्वरूपस्यतत्रानुप्रविष्टचिच्छायास्वरूप स्यचपृथक्करणमशक्यमितिभावः ॥ तदहंकारतादात्म्यात् तेनचिच्छायास हितेनाहंकारेणतादात्म्यात् सोहंकारआत्मानामस्वरूपं यस्यदेहस्यसतदा त्मातस्यभावस्तादात्म्यंसंबंधइत्यर्थः ॥ तस्मात्देहःस्थूलशरीरंस्वयंजडरूपमपि चेतनतांचेतनंज्ञानंतस्यभावश्चेतनतांज्ञानस्वरूपतामगात् प्राप्नुयादित्यर्थः ॥ यथापयसिपरीक्षणार्थंप्रक्षिप्तोमरकतमणिः पयोऽशेषमात्मच्छायंकुर्यान्न था

स्वभावतएवसर्वांतर : कूटस्थोसंगबोधरूप : साक्ष्यप्यहंकारादिस्थूलदेहप र्यंतमशेषंयुष्मदर्थमात्मच्छायंकुरुतइतिभाव: ॥७॥ नन्वेवमहंकारस्याचिच्छा यादेहाभ्यांतादात्म्येसत्यहंपश्याम्यहंशृणोमीत्यादेरनुभवसिध्धत्वात्।इंद्रियैरपि तादात्म्यमस्तीत्याशंक्य इंद्रियाणांस्वस्वगोलकस्थानमंतरेणस्वस्वविषयग्रहण सामर्थ्याभावात्।गोलकानांचस्थूलशरीरावयवत्वात् । अवयवावयविनोर्भेदा भावान्मनुष्योहंब्राह्मणोहंगृहस्थोहंकृष्णकेशोहमित्यादिवदहंचक्षुरहंश्रोत्रमि त्याद्यनुभवाभावात् ।कस्त्वमितिपृष्टेअहमितिवदतादेहस्यैवस्पृश्यमानत्वाच्चेंद्रि यतादात्म्यस्यापिदेहतादात्म्येंतर्भूतत्वात् पृथक्नेनिरूपणीयमित्यहंकारस्य संबंध्युद्देशद्वारेणतादात्म्यस्येयत्तांदर्शयति अहंकारस्येति ॥

अहंकारस्यतादात्म्यंचिच्छायादेहसाक्षिभिः ॥
सहजंकर्मजंभ्रांतिजन्यंचत्रिविधंक्रमात् ॥ ८ ॥

अहंकारस्येत्युक्तलक्षणस्यकर्तुश्चिच्छायादेहसाक्षीभि:चिच्छाययादेहेन साक्षिणाचसहक्रमात् संबंध्युद्देशक्रमेणत्रिविधंत्रिप्रकारंतादात्म्यं संबंधस्ते षांतादात्म्यानांसमर्थानिनामानिकल्पयति । सहजंचिच्छायाहंकारयोर्यत्तादा त्म्यंतत्संबंधिनोरुभयोरप्युत्पत्तिकालेसहैवजायतेइतिसहजमित्युच्यते । कर्म जमुक्तलक्षणाहंकारस्यचयत्तादात्म्यंतदन्वयव्यतिरेकाभ्यां जाग्रद्भोगप्रदकर्म णैवजायतेइतिकर्मजमित्युच्यते । भ्रांतिजन्यमधिष्ठानायाथात्म्यज्ञानंभ्रांति शब्देनोच्यते । अहंकारसाक्षिणोर्यत्तादात्म्यंतदनाद्यनिर्वचनीयभ्रांत्यैवजायत इतिभ्रांतिजन्यमित्युच्यते ॥ तादात्म्यत्रयसमुच्चयार्थश्चशब्दः । अत्रायंप्रयो ग: । अहंकारसाक्षिणोस्तादात्म्यंअधिष्ठानयाथात्म्याज्ञानजन्यं अधिष्ठान याथात्म्यज्ञानापनोद्यत्वात् यद्यदधिष्ठानयाथात्म्यज्ञानापनोद्यं तत्तदाधिष्ठान याथात्म्याज्ञानजन्यं यथारज्जुसर्पादिनांतादात्म्यंतथाचेदमधिष्ठानयाथा त्म्यज्ञानापनोद्यं तस्मादाधिष्ठानयाथात्म्याज्ञानजन्यमेवेति । एवमहंका रस्याचिच्छायादेहसाक्षिभिः संबंध्युद्देश्यक्रमेणैवोक्तलक्षणांत्रिविधंतादात्म्य मस्तीतिशेष : ॥ ९ ॥ ननुतर्हिउर्ध्वमूलमधःशाखमश्वत्थंप्राहुरव्ययमिति

एवमनादिरनंतोनैसर्गिकोयमितिच श्रीभगवद्भाष्यकाराभ्यामुक्तत्वादहंकारसाक्षिणोस्तादात्म्यस्यनिवृत्तिर्नास्ति । अतएवनिःशेषदुःखोच्छित्तिनिरतिशयानंदावाप्तिलक्षणमोक्षोप्याशामात्रमितिनशंक्यं ॥ ब्रह्मात्मज्ञानपर्यंतमेव भ्रांतिजन्यतादात्म्यस्याविनाशित्वेनताभ्यांविवक्षितत्वादन्यथास्ववाक्याविरोधात् सर्वेषांमोक्षशास्त्राणामप्रामाण्यप्रसंगाच्च मुमुक्षूणामपिसर्वेषांमोक्षविषयश्रवणादिप्रवृत्त्यभावाच्च कर्मजन्यतादात्म्यानिवृत्तेश्चप्रातिदिनंसुषुप्तावनुभूतत्वाच्च ॥ सहजतादात्म्यातिरिक्तयोरपितादात्म्ययोः स्वस्वकारणनाशद्वारानिवृत्तिरस्त्येव सहजतादात्म्यस्यतुसहजत्वादेवनिवृत्तिर्नास्तीत्याह संबंधीति ॥

संबंधिनःसतोर्नास्तिनिवृत्तिःसहजस्यतु ॥
कर्मक्षयात्प्रबोधाच्चनिवर्तेतेक्रमादुभे ॥९॥

संबंधिनोः सतोःपरस्परसंबंधित्वेनैवोत्पद्यमानयोरुत्पत्तिकालएवसंबंधिनोरित्यर्थः।तुशब्दोवधारणे ।सहजतादात्म्यस्येतरतादात्म्यवैलक्षण्यद्योतनार्थोवा । उक्तलक्षणयोश्चिच्छायाहंकारयोः सहजाख्यस्यतादात्म्यस्यनिवृत्तिर्नास्त्येव परस्परंपृथग्भावोनसंभवत्येव । सुषुप्तिमूर्छामरणादौजाग्रद्भोगप्रदकर्मक्षयात् जाग्रत्कालेश्रुत्याचार्यानुग्रहबलेनाहंब्रह्मास्मीति ब्रह्मात्मैक्यसाक्षात्काराच्चकर्मजन्यभ्रांतिजन्याख्ये उभेअपितादात्म्येनिमित्ताभावान्नैमित्तिकस्याप्यभाव इतिन्यायेनक्रमान्निवर्तेते । कर्मक्षयात् कर्मजंतादात्म्यंनिवर्त्तते । अहंकार देहाख्यावुभावपिसंबंधिनौपरस्परसंबंधंत्यजतइत्यर्थः । प्रबोधात् । अप्रबोध क्षयेसति भ्रांतिजन्यमपितादात्म्यंनिवर्तते बोधानंतरंसाक्षिसंबंधराहित्ये नाप्यहंकारप्रतीतिरन्यदृष्ट्यैवस्वदृष्ट्यानिवर्त्तते यथाशुक्तिकासमूहस्वरूपाज्ञानेननष्टेसतितत्रैवरजतंलीयते तथा स्वरूपपरिज्ञानात्स्वरूपापरिज्ञानेननष्टे सतिस्वस्मिन्नेवाहंकरोलीयत एव ॥९॥ संक्षेपेणावस्थात्रयस्वरूपमन्वयव्यतिरेकाभ्यांदेहस्याचेतनत्वंचदर्शयति अहंकारलयइति ॥

अहंकारलयेसुप्तौभवेद्देहोप्यचेतनः ॥
अहंकारविकासोर्धःस्वप्नःसर्वस्तुजागरः ॥१०॥

स्थूलसूक्ष्मभोगद्वयप्रदकर्मक्षयात्स्वकारणाज्ञानेऽहंकारेलीनेसतितदहंकार लयावस्था सुषुप्तिरित्युच्यते ॥ तस्यामवस्थायां पूर्वमहंकारसंबंधाच्चेतनत्वेनभातोदेहोप्यचेतनोभवेत् । अंधःसन्ननंधोभवतिविद्धःसन्नविद्धोभवतिउपतापीसन्ननुपतापीभवतीत्यादिश्रुतेः । अहंकृतिविकासार्द्धःस्वप्नः । सूक्ष्मभोगप्रदकर्मण्युद्बुद्धेसति तद्वशात्स्वकारणाज्ञानादुत्पन्नस्याहंकारस्य स्वव्यतिरिक्तवस्त्वंतराभावेपि जाग्रज्जनितसंस्कारमात्रस्वरूपभोगार्थस्थूलशरीरमंतरेणापि शरीरस्यांतःसूक्ष्मनाडीप्रचारोयःसएवतस्याहंकारस्यार्द्धविकासः । सएवस्वप्नइत्युच्यते । तत्राहंकारव्यतिरिक्तवस्त्वंतराभावेश्रुतिः । नतत्ररथानरथयोगानपंथानोभवंतीत्यादिः । सर्वस्तुजागरः । स्थूलभोगप्रदकर्मण्युद्बुद्धेसतितद्वशादापादमस्तकं स्थूलदेहेभिव्याप्तस्याहंकारस्यसर्वेन्द्रियैः सर्वविषयज्ञानं यत्सएवतस्याहंकारस्यपूर्णविकासस्तदेवजागरणमित्युच्यते । अस्यामवस्थायांपुनरहंकारसंबंधाद्देहःपूर्ववच्चेतनत्वेनानभासते । उभयत्राहंकारेसमानेस्वप्नाज्जागरितस्येंद्रियसद्भावात्मकवैलक्षण्यद्योतनार्थस्तुशब्दः । अत्रदर्शितेअवस्थात्रयलक्षणे मांडूक्यतापनीयाद्युपनिषदःप्रमाणयति दक्षिणाक्षिमुखेविश्वोमनस्यंतस्तुतैजसः आकाशेचहृदिप्राज्ञस्त्रिधादेहेप्रतिष्ठितइति । इंद्रियैरर्थोपलब्धिर्जागरितं । करणेषूपसंहृतेषु जागरितसंस्कारप्रत्ययविषयः स्वप्नः । सर्वप्रकारकज्ञानोपसंहारोबुद्धेः कारणात्मनावस्थानं सुषुप्तिरित्यादीनिश्रीमद्गौडपादाचार्यभगवत्पादाचार्यादिपूर्वाचार्यवचनानिच ॥ १० ॥ एवंकर्तृव्यापारं निरूप्य करणस्यापिक्रियाव्याप्यत्वंतात्क्रियांदर्शयति । अंतःकरणेति ।

अंतःकरणवृत्तिश्चचितिच्छायैक्यमागता ।
वासनाःकल्पयेत्स्वप्नेबोधेक्षैर्विषयान्बहिः ॥ ११ ॥

अंतःकरणंचासौवृत्तिश्चेत्यंतःकरणवृत्तिः । सच्चिदाभासकर्तृरूपवृत्तिमदपेक्षया करणभूतमनःशब्दवाच्याहमिदमात्मिकावृत्तिरितियावत् । वृत्तिश्चेति । चकारेणच्छायाहंकारैक्यविषयेप्रदर्शितोदृष्टांतादिरवस्थात्रयोप्यहंकारवत्संकोचविकासादिश्चात्रापिसमानइतिद्योत्यते । उक्तलक्षणासावृत्तिश्चसुषुप्तौ

लीयते।सापुनःसूक्ष्मभोगप्रदकर्मवशादुत्पत्तिसमयेचिच्छाययातप्तायःपिंडवदै क्यंप्राप्तासती स्वप्नावस्थायां नाडीमध्ये कर्तृकरणक्रियात्मकव्यवहारवासनाः कल्पयेत् । सैवपुनःस्थूलभोगप्रदकर्मवशात्स्थूलशरीरेणैक्यंप्राप्तासती जाग्रद वस्थायांश्रोत्रादींद्रियैःशब्दादिविषयान्बहिःकल्पयेत्।ननु बाह्यविषयाणामी श्वरस्रष्टृत्वेनांतःकरणकल्पितत्वमयुक्तमितिचेत् नैषदोषः। स्वरूपमात्रस्येश्व रस्रष्टृत्वेपि भोग्यत्वाकारस्यांतःकरणकरणकल्पितत्वात् । करणंकर्मकर्ताच क्रियास्वप्ने फलंचधीः जाग्रत्येवयतोदृष्टेत्याचार्यवचनाच्च ॥११॥ एवमे वांतःकरणं व्यवहारसौकर्यार्थमहंकारमनोभेदेनावयवशोविभज्य दर्शयित्वा इदानीमहंकारस्यापिमनोपेक्षयाकर्तृरूपत्वेपि चिच्छायावशतोबुद्धौ भानमि त्यत्रबुद्धिशब्देन निर्दिष्टांतःकरणाख्यद्रव्यापेक्षया करणत्वात् तस्यैवसर्वसं सारनिर्वाहकत्वेन मुख्यकर्तृत्वान्मुख्याहंकारत्वाच्च अहंकारमनोविभागपू र्वावस्थालक्षणस्य तस्यांतःकरणाख्यद्रव्यस्य स्वरूपंदर्शयति । मनोहंकृतीति।

मनोहंकृत्युपादानंलिंगमेकंजडात्मकं ।
अवस्थात्रयमन्वेति जायते म्रियते तथा ॥१२॥

मनोहंकृत्योरुपादानंकारणंयत्तन्मनोहंकृत्युपादानं।किंतत्।लिंगं लिंग्यते गम्यतेऽनेनेतिलिंगमंतःकरणाख्यं द्रव्यमित्यर्थः । तस्यैवाहंब्रह्मास्मीत्यखंडा कारवृत्तिद्वारेण सच्चिदानंदाद्वितीयब्रह्मात्मगमकत्वात् । ननुतत्वविवेकाख्ये ग्रंथेबुध्धिकर्मेंद्रियप्राणपंचकैर्मनसाधियाशरीरंसप्तदशभिः सूक्ष्मंतल्लिंगमुच्यते इतिसप्तदशावयवात्मकस्य सूक्ष्मशरीरस्यैवलिंगत्वमुक्तं नांतःकरणस्यलिंगत्वमु पपद्यतेइत्याशंक्य बुध्धिकर्मेंद्रियप्राणपंचकानां वेदांतेषु भौतिकत्वेन श्रुतत्वेपि अन्यत्रमनाअभूवंनादर्शमन्यत्रमनाअभूवंनाश्रौषमित्यादिश्रुतिष्वंतःकरणाधी नत्वश्रवणात्।अतएवअहंकारमनःसहितानां तेषांज्ञानक्रियाशक्तिद्वयात्मकांतः करणवृत्तित्वात।वृत्ति वृत्तिमतोर्व्यावहारिकभेदविवक्षया तत्रोक्तत्वात् ।तयोः पारमार्थिकाभेदविवक्षयैवात्रोक्तत्वात्।तद्विवक्षाभेदेनपक्षभेदेनपक्षद्वयस्याप्य नुपपन्नत्वात्।उक्तलक्षणस्यांतःकरणस्य सूक्ष्मशरीरत्वं लिंगत्वं चोपपद्यतएवे

त्यभिप्रायेणाह एकमिति । एवमुक्तलक्षणमंतःकरणं स्वभावतोजडमप्यनुःप्रविष्टचिच्छायाबलेनैवस्थूलशरीरमपि आत्मत्वेनैवगृहीत्वा पूर्वोक्तसंकोचःविकासप्रकारेणानुदिनमवस्थात्रयं प्राप्नोति ॥ यथाकर्म्मवशादवस्थात्रयंप्राप्नोःति तथाजननमरणादिकं च कर्मवशात्प्राप्नोतीत्यर्थः॥ जायतेम्रियतइत्युक्त्वानंतरं तथाशब्दप्रयोक्तुर्धर्माधर्मवशात्घटीयंत्रवत्पौनःपुन्येनजन्ममरणेप्राप्नोतीत्यभिप्रायः।शोकहर्षभयक्रोधलोभमोहस्पृहादयःअहंकारस्य दृश्यंते जन्ममृत्युश्चनात्मनः।एवं दुःखाद्यनुभवन्संसारेऽस्मिन्पुमान्मुने।घटीयंत्रवदुद्विग्नोजायतेम्रियतेचसः इत्यादिपुराणवचनाच्च॥ १२॥एवंनिखिलसंसारनिर्वाहकलिंगशरीरस्वरूपंनिरूप्येदानीमस्य लिंगस्य विराडंतसमस्तप्रपंचस्य मूलकारणभूतायाःसच्चिदानंदब्रह्माश्रयाया अविद्याऽज्ञानतमोमोहादिशब्दवाच्यायाःसर्वानर्थबीजभूताया अनिर्वचनीयाया मायायाःस्वरूपंतच्छक्तिद्वारेणविभज्य दर्शयितुं तच्छक्तेरियत्तांतावद्दर्शयति । शक्तिद्वयमिति ।

शक्तिद्वयंहिमायायाःविक्षेपावृत्तिरूपकं ।
विक्षेपशक्तिर्लिंगादिब्रह्मांडांतंजगत्सृजेत् ॥१३॥

उक्तलक्षणाया मायायाआवरणशक्तिर्विक्षेपशक्तिरितिद्वयमस्तीतिशेषः।जीवेशावाभासेनकरोतिमाया चाविद्याचस्वयमेवभवतीत्यादिवेदांतवाक्येषुमायायाःशक्तिद्वयात्मत्वंप्रसिद्धमितिशास्त्रप्रसिद्धिंद्योतयतिहिशब्दः।अधिष्ठानमनाच्छाद्य विक्षेपयितुमशक्यत्वेन विक्षेपशक्तेरावरणशक्तिपूर्वकत्वादावरणशक्तेरग्रत्वेपिछंदोभंगभयाद्विक्षेपशब्दपूर्वनिपातः कृतः। एवंशक्तेरियत्तामुक्त्वेदानींसच्चिदानंदलक्षणब्रह्मात्मस्वरूपमात्राच्छादिकायाः विक्षेपशक्त्याभिव्यक्तेः पूर्वावस्थालक्षणायाआवरणशक्तेःसर्वानर्थबीजत्वेनाग्रत्वेपिविक्षेपशक्तेर्नैरपेक्ष्येण ब्रह्मानंदानुभवांतिरस्कृत्य सांसारिकसुखदुःखादिभोगप्रदत्वसामर्थ्याभावात् प्रतिदिनंसुषुप्तावनुभूतत्वेनअस्मिन्नर्थे नकस्यापिविप्रतिपत्तिसंभवात् विक्षेपशक्त्यभिव्यक्त्यनंतरतया सृष्टस्याहंकारादिदेहांतस्य युष्मदर्थस्यशरीरत्रयविलक्षण

स्य कूटस्थासंगबोधरूपस्य साक्षिणश्चस्वभावसिद्धं भेदंसैवावरणशक्तिर्येनांशे नावृणोति तस्यैवांशस्य सुखित्वदुःखित्वाद्यनेकविधसंसारकारणत्वात् तादृशा वरणशक्त्यंशस्योक्तरीत्या विक्षेपशक्त्यनंतरभावित्वात् तदपेक्षयाविक्षेपशक्तेर ग्रत्वादनेनैवाभिप्रायेणावरणशक्तिस्वरूपंपश्चान्निरूपयिष्यन् विक्षेपशक्तिस्व रूपंतावन्निरूपयति । विविधंकरणंविक्षेपः विविधंभवनंवा साचासौशक्ति श्चेतिविक्षेपशक्तिः । अध्यात्मविश्वतैजसप्राज्ञादिभेदेनाधिदैवतंविराट्हिरण्य गर्भांतरयाम्यादिभेदेनचस्वगतादिभेदरहितं चिन्मात्रं विक्षेपयतीतिविक्षेपश क्तिः। उक्तलक्षणंचिन्मात्रमनयाविक्षिप्यतइति वा गिरिनदीसमुद्राद्यनेकनाम रूपाकारेण स्वयमेवविक्षिपाति नामरूपाद्याकारेणपरिणमते विवर्त्ततइत्यर्थः।एव मिति वा विक्षेपशक्तिर्जायतेपुनर्लयंगच्छतीति जगदुक्तलक्षणासाशक्तिरुक्तलक्ष णंसमष्टिव्यष्ट्यात्मकंलिंगशरीरादिब्रह्मांडांतंजगत्सृजेदुत्पादयेदित्यर्थः ॥ ॥१३॥एवंविक्षेपशक्तिस्वरूपंनिरूप्यतद्व्यापारात्मकसृष्टिस्वरूपंद्वारेणापितदे वविशदयति । सृष्टिर्नामेति ।

सृष्टिर्नामब्रह्मरूपे सच्चिदानंदवस्तुनि ।
अब्धौफेनादिवत्सर्वनामरूपप्रसारणम् ॥१४॥

ब्रह्मस्वरूपे सच्चिदानंदवस्तुन्यारोपितनामरूपयोरवस्तुत्वादधिष्ठानस्य तद्वत्वे लक्षण्यं द्योतयतिच तुशब्दः।सच्चिदानंदश्चतद्वस्तुचेतिसच्चिदानंदवस्तु तस्मि न्परमार्थसच्चिदानंदलक्षणेब्रह्मणीत्यर्थः नामचरूपंचनामरूपेसर्वेचतेनामरूपे च तयोः प्रसारणंविस्तारःविततिःसृष्टिरित्युच्यते।एतदुक्तंभवति ब्रह्मण्यवस्थि तायाःविक्षेपाऽऽत्मिकाया मायायास्तस्मिन्नेवब्रह्मणिसमस्तनामरूपाकारेण विवर्त्तनंयत्सैवसृष्टिरित्युच्यतइति। अत्रदृष्टांतमाह अब्धौफेनादिवदिति । अ ब्धाववस्थिताया विक्षेपात्मिकाया मायायास्तत्रैवफेनतरंग बुद्बुदाद्याकारेण विवर्त्तनंयथासृष्टिशब्देनोच्यते तथात्रापीतिभावः ॥ १४ ॥ एवंविक्षेपश क्तिद्वारामायास्वरूपंदर्शयित्वावरणशक्तिद्वारेणापितदेवदर्शयति । अंतरिति।

अंतर्दृग्दृश्ययोर्भेदं बहिश्च ब्रह्मसर्गयोः ।

आवृणोत्यपराशक्तिः सासंसारस्यकारणं ॥ १५ ॥

अंतःस्थूलशरीरस्यांतर्देशे दृग्दृश्ययोर्भेदं अहमन्नादोहमन्नाद इत्यादिश्रु त्यनुसारेण शरीरत्रयतादात्म्यवशात् भोक्तृत्वमापन्नस्य परमार्थतस्तद्राहितस्य केवलदृङ्मात्रस्वरूपस्यास्मदर्थस्यसाक्षिणः अविद्याकार्यत्वेन जडरूपस्याहंकारादिदेहांतस्य युष्मदर्थस्यच भेदं अन्योन्यवैलक्षण्यं अन्योन्यपृथग्भावं। बहिः शरीरस्यबाह्यदेशे ब्रह्मसर्गयोर्भेदं सच्चत्यच्चाभवत् अहमन्नमहमन्नमित्यादिश्रुत्यनुसारेण नामरूपतादात्म्यवशात् भोग्यत्वमापन्नस्य परमार्थतस्तद्राहितस्यपरब्रह्मण स्तस्मिं च्छुक्तिकायां रजतवदध्यस्तनामरूपात्मकस्य सर्गस्यच भेदं।एव मंतरुक्तलक्षणयोर्दृग्दृश्ययोर्भेदं बहिर्ब्रह्मसर्गयोर्भेदंचापराशक्तिः पूर्वोक्तरीत्या विक्षेपशक्त्यनंतरभावित्वेपि स्वरूपतो विक्षेपशक्तिप्रवर्तकत्वेन तत्कारणभूतावरणशब्दवाच्यामायाशक्तिरावृणोति आच्छादयति।सा संसारस्यकारणं।अंतर्दृक्स्वरूपस्यसाक्षिणःकर्तृत्वभोक्तृत्वादिलक्षणस्यसंसारस्यसैवकारणं तस्याएवान्योन्याध्यासहेतुत्वेनसर्वानर्थकारित्वादितिभावः । बहिःसच्चिदानंदलक्षणस्य ब्रह्मणोभोग्यत्वादिविकारस्यापिसैवकारणमित्यर्थाल्लभ्यते भोक्तृत्वस्यभोग्यापेक्षत्वात् ॥ १५ ॥ एवंशक्तिद्वयात्मकंमायास्वरूपंप्रदर्श्येदानींप्रकृतानुसारेणमनोहंकृत्युपादानमित्यस्मिन्श्लोकेसामान्यतोदर्शितंलिंगस्वरूपं विशेषतः प्रदर्शयति । साक्षिणइति ।

साक्षिणः पुरतो भातं लिंगं देहेनसंयुतम् ।

चितिच्छायासमावेशाज्जीवःस्याद्व्यावहारिकः ॥१६॥

चितिच्छायासमावेशात् अनुप्रविष्टचैतन्यबलात् साक्षिणःप्रत्यगात्मनः पुरतःअग्रतःकर्मत्वेनेतियावत् भातंभासमानं देहेनसंयुतं स्थूलशरीरेणैक्यप्राप्तंलिंगं पूर्वोक्तलक्षणं लिंगशरीरं जीवः स्याद्व्यावहारिकः । लोकद्वयेपिप्रमात्रादिसमस्तव्यवहारनिर्वाहकत्वाद्व्यावहारिकाख्योजीवः स्यात्।अस्यानिर्वचनीयत्वा

याकार्यत्वेनप्रकृतिलक्षणविकारित्वात् सकलसंसारानिर्वाहकत्वात् सच्चिदानंदब्रह्मात्मैक्यस्वरूपावस्थानलक्षणमोक्षदशायाप्रभावाच्चव्यावहारिकजीवइत्युक्तं। ॥१६॥ननुव्यावहारिकजीवस्यसकलसंसारानिर्वाहकत्वेपि मिथ्याभूतत्वात् नित्यमुक्तस्यसाक्षिणःसंसाराभावाच्च उभयोरपिमोक्षानधिकारादन्यस्याचेदधिकारिणोऽभावाच्चमोक्षशास्त्रवैयर्थ्यंस्यादित्यतआह । अस्येति ।

अस्यजीवत्वमारोपात्साक्षिण्यप्यवभासते ।

आवृत्तौतुविनष्टायांभेदेभातेपयातितत् ॥ १७ ॥

अस्यव्यावहारिकजीवस्य जीवत्वं जीवभावःआरोपात् आवरणकशक्तिकृतादन्योन्याध्यासात् साक्षिण्यपि दृग्रूपेप्रत्यगात्मन्यपि जीवत्वं साक्षिणिप्रत्यगात्मनिपरमार्थतोजीवत्वासंभवंद्योतयत्यपिशब्दः अवभासतेप्रकाशते ।स्वरूपचैतन्यावगतित्वेन भासतेइतिभावः। तुशब्दोवधारणे । आवृत्तावसत्वावृत्तिरूपेणाभानावृत्तिरूपेण चद्विप्रकारमायावरणशक्तौ अहंब्रह्मास्मीत्यखंडैकरसब्रह्मात्मसाक्षात्कारेण विनष्टायां विशेषेणनष्टायांसत्यां पुनर्भ्रांत्यनुदयोनाशस्यविशेषःआत्यंतिकनाशंप्राप्तायामित्यर्थः । भेदेभाते व्यावहारिकजीवस्वरूपस्यलिंगशरीरस्यघटादिवद्दृश्यत्वं । प्रत्यग्बोधस्वरूपस्यसाक्ष्याख्यस्यस्वस्यद्रष्टृत्वंच भेदस्तस्मिन्सम्यक्प्रकाशितेसति साक्षिण्यारोपितंतज्जीवत्वमपयात्यपगच्छत्येवेत्यत्रतुशब्दःसंबध्यतेयस्मादेवंतस्माच्छास्त्रवैयर्थ्यंनस्यादित्यभिप्रायः ॥१७॥यथाव्यावहारिकजीवगतंजीवत्वमारोपात्साक्षिण्यप्यवभासते तथानामरूपात्मकःसर्वगतोविकारः आरोपाद्ब्रह्मण्यप्यवभासतइत्याह । तथेति ।

तथासर्गब्रह्मणोश्चभेदमावृत्यतिष्ठति ।

याशक्तिस्तद्वशाद्ब्रह्मविकृतत्वेनभासते ॥ १८ ॥

यथा अंतःदृग्दृश्यभेदमाच्छादयति तथासर्गब्रह्मणोर्भेदंचावृत्यावरणशक्तिस्तिष्ठति तद्वशात् तदावरणशक्तिकृतादन्योन्याध्यासवशात् ब्रह्म सच्चिदानंदलक्षणः परमात्मा विकृतत्वेनभासते स्वयंकूटस्थमपिषड्भावविकारशून्य

मपितद्रूत्वेनभासतइत्यर्थः ॥१८॥ ब्राह्मेप्यावृत्तिनाशेनसर्गब्रह्मभेदस्फुरणात् ब्रह्मण्यारोपितोविकारोनिवर्त्ततइत्याह । अत्रापीति

अत्राप्यावृत्तिनाशेनविभातिब्रह्मसर्गयोः ।
भेदस्तयोर्विकारःस्यात्सर्गेनब्रह्मणिक्वचित् ॥ १९ ॥

अत्रापि यथा तथाब्राह्मेप्यावृत्तिनाशेनान्वयव्यतिरेकाभ्यामंतर्बहिश्चपदार्थद्वयपरिशोधनपूर्वकेणाहंब्रह्मास्मीत्यभिव्यक्तेन सच्चिदानंदलक्षणब्रह्मात्मबोधेनउक्तलक्षणायामावरणशक्तौवासनयासहविनष्टायांसत्यां तेनावृत्तिनाशेनब्रह्मसर्गयोर्भेदोविभाति घटपटयोरिवभेदःसम्यक्प्रकाशते।एवंभेदेभातेसति तयोः ब्रह्मसर्गयोर्मध्येनामरूपात्मकेसर्गेएवजन्मादिविकारः स्यात्नब्रह्मणिक्वचित्। आनंदलक्षणेब्रह्मण्येकदेशेपिविकारोनस्यादित्यर्थः॥१९॥एवमंतर्बहिश्चावृत्तिकार्यतादात्म्यवशात्साक्षिब्रह्मणोभोक्तृत्वभोग्यत्वादिरूपाविकारंतदावृत्तिनाशेन तत्कृतविकारनिवृत्तिंचदर्शयित्वा इदानींब्रह्मणःसर्वात्मकत्वदर्शनद्वारेण त्वंपदार्थमप्यर्थाद्विवेचयन्मुख्यतस्तत्पदार्थंविविनक्ति। अस्तिभातीति।

अस्तिभातिप्रियंरूपंनामचेत्यंशपंचकं ।
आद्यंत्रयंब्रह्मरूपंजगद्रूपंततोद्वयं ॥ २०॥

अस्तिविद्यते भातिप्रकाशते प्रियंप्रेमास्पदं रूपजगद्रूपपृथुबुध्नोदरोतप्रोतादिकं नामघटः पटइत्यादिकं एतत्सर्वंमिलित्वांशपंचकमिदमेकंवस्तुअस्तीदंभातीदं प्रियमिदमस्यरूपमिदमस्यनामेतिएतदंशपंचकव्यतिरेकेणव्यवहारासंभवाल्लोकव्यवहारगोचरभूतभौतिकात्मकंसमस्तंवस्त्वपिसच्चिदानंदरूपनामलक्षणांशपंचात्मकमेवभवतीतियावत्।अंशपंचकसमुच्चयार्थश्चशब्दः। एतेष्वंशेषुमध्येआद्यत्रयं सच्चिदानंदात्मकमंशत्रयं ब्रह्मरूपंब्रह्मस्वरूपं ततोद्वयंतस्मात्सच्चिदानंदात्मकांशत्रयादुपरितननामरूपात्मकमंशद्वयंजगद्रूपमित्यर्थः॥२०॥ उक्तमेवार्थमन्वयव्यतिरेकाभ्यांस्पष्टयति।खवाय्विति।

खवाय्वग्निजलोर्वीषुदेवतिर्यङ्नरादिषु ।
अभिन्नाः सच्चिदानंदा भिद्येते रूपनामनी ॥ २१ ॥

आकाशवायुतेजोम्बवन्याख्येषुपंचभूतेषुदेवतिर्यङ्नरादिभेदभिन्नेषुशरीरलक्षणेषु भौतिकेषु वर्तमानाः सच्चिदानंदाः त्रयोप्यंशाअभिन्नानिर्विशेषाः स्युः घटोस्ति पटोस्ति घटोभाति पटोभाति घटःप्रियः पटःप्रियः इतिसर्वत्रानुवृत्तस्वभावत्वात् रूपनामनी भूतेषुभौतिकेषुचवर्तमानौरूपनामात्मकावुभावप्यंशौ भिद्येते ॥ईदृग्रूपस्तादृग्रूपोघटःपटइत्यादिभेदभिन्नत्वेनवर्तेते ॥ अनिर्वचनीयमायाकार्यत्वेनव्यावृत्तस्वभावत्वात् ॥२१॥ एवंप्राक्तनग्रंथसंदर्भेणान्वयव्यतिरेकाभ्यांपदार्थद्वयं परिशोध्येदानींनामरूपोपेक्षापुरःसरंसच्चिदानंदेतत्परोभूत्वा वाक्यश्रवणांगत्वेनवाक्यार्थज्ञानसाधनभूतं वक्ष्यमाणभेदभिन्नंसमाधिंहृदयेवाबाह्येवानिरंतरंकुर्यादित्याह । उपेक्ष्येति ॥

उपेक्ष्यनामरूपेद्वेसच्चिदानंदतत्परः
समाधिंसर्वदाकुर्याध्द्रदयेचाथवाबहिः ॥ २२ ॥

जगद्रूपेनामरूपेद्वेउपेक्ष्यावज्ञायोदासीनीकृत्य सच्चिदानंदतत्परःसच्चिदानंदरूपब्रह्मात्मन्येवतात्पर्यवान् तदेकचित्तइत्यर्थः तादृशोभूत्वा समाधिंवक्ष्यमाणंचित्तसमाधानं सर्वेंद्रियाण्यपिहृदयकमलेनिरुध्यतत्रतत्रवागादींद्रियाणांस्वस्वगोलकावस्थानेपितेषांवृत्तिमात्रं निरुध्य शरीरादंतर्बाह्यदेशेचवक्ष्यमाणप्रकारेणानिरंतरंकुर्यादित्यर्थः।विधिमुखतः समाधिंविधायानेनश्लोकेनप्रतिपादितपदंप्रतिपरमहंसस्यैवब्रह्मज्ञानाधिकारोनान्यस्येतिसूचयति॥२२॥एवंब्रह्मजिज्ञासुमुमुक्षुंप्रतिनिदिध्यासितव्यइत्येतद्वाक्यानुसारेणावश्यकर्त्तव्यत्वेनसमाधिंविधायेदानींतस्यसमाधेरवांतरभेदंदर्शयन्नेतान्समाधीन्हृदयेकुर्यादित्याह सविकल्पइति ।

सविकल्पोनिर्विकल्पः समाधिर्द्विविधोहृदि ।
दृश्यसब्दानुविध्धेनसविकल्पः पुनर्द्विधा ॥ २३ ॥

सविकल्पसमाधिर्निर्विकल्पसमाधिरितिसमाधिर्द्विविधोद्विप्रकारोभवेत् दृश्यानुविद्धः सविकल्पकः शब्दानुविद्धः सविकल्पइति सविकल्पसमाधिरपि द्विप्रकारोभवेत्।एवमुक्तप्रकारेणदृश्यानुविद्धःसविकल्पसमाधिःशब्दानुविद्धः सविकल्पसमाधिर्निर्विकल्पकश्चेति त्रिप्रकारं समाधिं क्रमेण हृदयेकुर्यादितिशेषः ।दृश्यमिश्रोदृश्यानुविद्धः शब्दमिश्रः शब्दानुविद्धः ॥२३॥ सविकल्पोनिर्विकल्पश्चेतिसविकल्पस्यप्रथमोद्दिष्टत्वात् तत्रापिदृश्यशब्दानुविद्धश्चेति दृश्यानुविद्धस्यैवप्रथमोद्दिष्टत्वात् अंतर्दृग्दृश्यविवेकं दृगेकनिष्ठंदृश्यानुविद्धंसविकल्पसमाधिं तावद्दर्शयति । कामाद्याइति ।

कामाद्याश्चित्तगादृश्यास्तत्साक्षित्वेनचेतनं ।
ध्यायेद्दृश्यानुविद्धोयंसमाधिःसविकल्पकः ॥ २४ ॥

कामाद्याःकामसंकल्पादयःपूर्वोक्ताश्चित्तगाः अंतःकरणवृत्तित्वेनांतःकरणनिष्ठा दृश्याःकार्यभूताःयुष्मत्प्रत्ययविषयाभवंतीतिशेषः। तत्साक्षित्वेनतेष कामादिचित्तगतदृश्यानां प्रकाशकत्वेन चेतनमात्मानं प्रत्यक्चैतन्यंध्यायेत्। एतदुक्तंभवति तेषांकामादिनांमध्येएकमेकंप्रतियोगिनंकृत्वास्यकामस्यय त्साक्षिभूतंचैतन्यंतदेव मम याथात्म्यंस्वरूपमेवंनिरंतरंप्रत्यग्रूपं चिन्मात्रंभावयेदिति । एवमुक्तप्रकारेणचिन्मात्रेभावितेसति अयंदृश्यानुविद्धःसविकल्पकसमाधिरित्युच्यतइतिशेषः । नमेस्याद्विक्रियांदुःखसाक्षिताकाविकारिणः धीविक्रियासहस्राणांसाक्षितोहमविक्रियःइतिनैष्कर्म्यसिद्धिकारस्मरणात् ॥ २४ ॥एवंदृश्यप्रतियोगिकंसविकल्पसंज्ञकंसमाधिंदर्शयित्वाइदानींक्रमप्राप्तंकामाद्यशेषदृश्यविलापकंसाक्षिनिष्ठंशब्दानुविध्धंसविकल्पसमाधिंदर्शयति । असंगइति ।

असंगःसच्चिदानंदःस्वप्रभोद्वैतवर्जितः ।
अस्मीतिशब्दाविद्धोयंसमाधिःसविकल्पकः ॥२५॥

असंगः संगरहितः असंगोह्ययंपुरुषः । स्वप्रभः स्वयंप्रकाशः अदृष्टंदृष्टृ श्रुतंश्रोतृनदृष्टेर्द्रष्टारंपश्येदित्यादिश्रुतेः । द्वैतवर्जितः प्रकाश्यस्यप्रकाशाभिन्नत्वेनकामाद्यशेषरहितःस्वगतादिभेदराहितइत्यर्थःएकमेवाद्वितीयमितिश्रुतेः। एवमुक्तलक्षणःप्रत्यग्रूपोयः साक्षी सोऽयमहमस्मीतिनिरंतरंभावयेत् ।एवंमुक्तप्रकारेणकामाद्यशेषवृत्तिविलापको ऽसंगादिशब्दमात्रमिश्रितोविजातीयप्रत्ययशून्यसजातीयप्रत्ययप्रवाहलक्षणप्रत्यकूचिन्मात्रनिष्ठोयोनुभवः सोऽयंशब्दानुविद्धःसविकल्पसमाधिरित्युच्यतइतिशेषः । निरीहोस्मिनिरंशोस्मिस्वस्थोस्म्यस्मिचनिस्पृहः शांतोहमर्थरूपोस्मिचिरायाहमलंस्थितइतिवशिष्ठवचनात् ॥ २९ ॥ एवंद्विप्रकारंसविकल्पसमाधिंदर्शयित्वा इदानीं कामादिदृश्यानामसंगादिशब्दानां विलापकंनिवातस्थितदीपवच्चित्तनैश्चल्यात्मकंनिर्विकल्पसमाधिंदर्शयति । स्वानुभूतिरिति ।

स्वानुभूतिरसावेशाद्दृश्यशब्दानुपेक्षितुः ।
निर्विकल्पःसमाधिःस्यान्निवातस्थितदीपवत् ॥ २६ ॥

अनुभूतिर्ज्ञानंप्रत्यकूचैतन्यं यानुभूतिरजामेयास्वनंतानंदविग्रहा महदादिजगन्मायाचित्रभित्तिंनमामितां इतिइष्टसिद्धिकारैरुक्तत्वात् । रसआनंदस्वरूपः परमात्मा रसोवैसः रसंह्येवायंलब्ध्वानंदीभवतीतिश्रुतेः । प्रत्यगात्मापिरसाभिन्नत्वेनपरप्रेमास्पदत्वाद्रसः स्वरूपभूताऽनुभूतिरेवरसस्तस्यावेशः स्वानुभूतिरसावेशः। पूर्वोक्तसमाधिद्वयाभ्यासपाटवादंतःकरणेस्वरूपभूतज्ञानानंदाविर्भावः स्वानुभूतिरसावेशइत्युच्यते । यद्वाआवेशोभिनिवेशः मग्नत्वंस्वानुभूतिरसावेशः। यद्वा आसमंतात्प्रवेशः आवेशः स्वरूपज्ञानानंदपूर्णत्वं। यद्वा देवताद्यावेशवत्स्वानुभूतिरसावेशस्तस्मात्स्वानुभूतिरसावेशात् ।स्वानुभूतिरसास्वादादितिपाठेसच्चिदानंदस्वरूपोहमितिस्वानुभूतिरसस्यात्मत्वेनस्वीकरणंस्वानुभूतिरसास्वादस्तस्मात्।दृश्यशब्दानुपेक्षितुःपूर्वोक्तान्कामादिदृश्यानसंगादिशब्दांश्चोपेक्षितुरुदासीनकर्तृत्वभयत्रतःपर्यराहित्येन तुष्णींस्थितस्य देवताद्याविष्टवत्स्वानुभूतिरसाख्यमहाग्रहग्रस्तत्वेनस्वातंत्र्याभावात्परतंत्रतयास्थित

स्येतितात्पर्यार्थोनिर्विकल्पः समाधिःस्यात् । प्रशांतवृत्तिकंचित्तंपरमानन्ददीपकं असंप्रज्ञातनामायंसमाधिर्योगिनांप्रियइति।उक्तलक्षणोनिर्विकल्पः समाधि रुक्तलक्षणस्याऽधिकारिणःस्वयमेवस्यात् लयविक्षेपकषायादिमतिबंधाभावादसंप्रज्ञाताख्योनिर्विकल्पसमाधिःस्वयमेवभवतीत्यर्थः। तस्मिन्समाधौचित्तनैश्चल्येदृष्टांतमाह निवातस्थितदीपवदिति । निवातस्थलेस्थापितोदीपोयथानिश्चलोभवतितथासमप्राप्तंचित्तमपिनिश्चलंभवतीत्यर्थः तत्परंपुरुषख्यातेर्गुणवैतृष्ण्यं तीव्रसंवेगानामासन्नःसमाधिलाभः व्युत्थाननिरोधसंस्कारयोरभिभवप्रादुर्भावौनिरोधक्षणचित्तान्वयोनिरोधपरिणामइतिपतंजलिनासूत्रितत्वात् । यथादीपोनिवातस्थोनेंगतेसोपमास्मृता योगिनोयतचित्तस्ययुंजतोयोगमात्मनइत्यादिभगवद्वचनात् ।अंतःशून्योबहिःशून्यःशून्यकुंभइवांबरे अंतःपूर्णोबहिःपूर्णःपूर्णकुंभइवार्णवे माभवग्राह्यभावात्माग्राहकात्माचमाभव भावनामखिलांत्यक्त्वायादिष्टंतन्मयोभव द्रष्टृदर्शनदृश्यानित्यक्त्वावासनयासह दर्शनंप्रथमाभ्यासमात्मानंकेवलंभज प्रशांतसर्वसंकल्पायाशिलावदवस्थितिः जाग्रन्निद्राविनिर्मुक्तासास्वरूपस्थितिःपरा इतिवशिष्ठवचनाच्च । अस्यसमाधेर्वाक्यश्रवणांगत्वं चतत्वविवेकाख्येग्रंथेश्रीमद्विद्यारण्यगुरुभिर्निरूपितं अमुनावासनाजालेनिःशेषंप्रविलापिते समूलोन्मूलितेपुण्यपापाख्येकर्मसंचये वाक्यमप्रतिबद्धंसत्प्राक्परोक्षावभासिते करामलकवद्बोधमपरोक्षंप्रसूयतइति ॥ २६ ॥ एवंहृदयसंबंधित्वेनदर्शितंत्रिप्रकारमिमंसमाधिंबाह्यसंबंधित्वेनापिदर्शयिषुःबहिःब्रह्मसर्गविवेकंसच्चिदानंदलक्षणब्रह्मनिष्ठं दृश्यानुविद्धं समाधितावद्दर्शयति । हृदीवेति ।

हृदीवबाह्यदेशेपियस्मिन्कस्मिंश्चवस्तुनि ।
समाधिराद्यःसन्मात्रान्नामरूपपृथक्कृतिः ॥ २७ ॥

यथाहृदयेसाक्षिणःसकाशात्कामादीनांपृथक्करणमाद्यःसमाधिः। एतदुक्तंभवतियथाहृदिकामादीनांमध्येएकमेकंप्रतियोगिनंकृत्वास्वात्मनःसकाशान्नामरूपयोः पृथक्करणमस्यसाक्षिभूतंयच्चैतन्यंतदेवाहमस्मि अस्यसंकल्पस्य

साक्षिभूतंयच्चैतन्यं तदेवाहमस्मि इत्यनुचिंतनंदृश्यानुविद्धसमाधिरि त्युच्यते तथाबाह्योपिस्वाभीष्टमेकंवस्त्ववलंब्यांशपंचकेतस्मिन्वस्तुनिवर्त्त मानात्सच्चिदानंदलक्षणब्रह्मणःसकाशात् नामरूपेपृथक्कृत्वानयोःपृथक्कृत योः नामरूपयोरधिष्ठानभूतंसच्चिदानंदलक्षणंयद्वस्तुतदेवतत्पदलक्ष्यंब्रह्मेत्यनु चिंतनं दृश्यानुविद्धसमाधिरित्युच्यतइति यत्रस्थितेयंविश्वश्रीः प्रतिभामा त्ररूपिणी रज्ज्वांभुजंगवद्भातिसोयमात्मासदोदितइतिवशिष्ठवचनाच्च॥२७॥ एवंदृश्यानुविद्धंसमाधिंनिरूप्येदानींसमष्टिव्यष्ट्यात्मकसमस्तदृश्यप्रपंचवि लापकंशब्दानुविध्धसमाधिंनिरूपयति । अखंडैकरसमिति ।

अखंडैकरसंवस्तुसच्चिदानंदलक्षणं ।
इत्यविच्छिन्नचिंतेयंसमाधिर्मध्यमोभवेत् ॥ २८ ॥

अखंडंदेशकालाद्यपरिच्छिन्नंस्वगतादिभेदरहितमितियावत् एकमेवाद्वि तीयमितिश्रुतेः नव्यापित्वाद्देशतोंतोनित्यत्वान्नापिकालतः नवस्तुतोपिसा र्वात्म्यादानंत्यंब्रह्मणित्रिधा इतितैरेवपंचकोशविवेकाख्येग्रंथउपपत्तिभिरखं डत्वस्यसमर्थितत्वाच्च । एकरसंकालत्रयेप्येकरूपं कूटस्थमित्यर्थः अव्यक्तोय मचिंत्योयमविकार्योयमुच्यतइतिभगवद्वचनात् । अखंडंचतदेकरसंचेत्यखं डैकरसं । सच्चिदानंदलक्षणंस्पष्टार्थः । एवमुक्तलक्षणंयद्वस्तुतदेवब्रह्मेत्यवि च्छिन्नचिंताविजातीयप्रत्ययानंतरितसजातीयप्रत्ययप्रवाहरूपा या चिंतासायं मध्यमः समाधिर्भवेत् शब्दानुविद्धसविकल्पसमाधिर्भवेदित्यर्थः।एवंब्रह्मचिदा काशंसर्वात्मकमखंडितं नीरंध्रभूरिवाशेषमितिभावयराघव नाहंनचान्यद्वा स्तीतिब्रह्मैवास्मिनिरंतरं आनंदपूर्णःसर्वत्राप्यनुद्वेगादुपास्यतामितिवशिष्ठवच नात् ॥ २९ ॥ एवंब्रह्मविषयंद्विप्रकारंसविकल्पसमाधिंनिरूप्येदानींपूर्वोक्त समस्तदृश्यशब्दविलापकनिर्विकल्पसमाधिप्रदर्शनपूर्वकमुक्तलक्षणैरेतैः ष ड्भिःसमाधिभिर्निरंतरंकालंनयेदित्याह । स्तब्धीभावइति ।

स्तब्धीभावोरसास्वादात्तृतीयःपूर्ववन्मतः ।
एतैःसमाधिभिःषड्भिर्नयेत्कालंनिरंतरं ॥ २९ ॥

रसशब्दोव्याख्यातः। आंतरस्यत्रिप्रकारस्यसमाधेर्विषयभूतस्यसाक्षिणः साक्षित्वसिद्ध्यर्थं ब्रह्माभिन्नत्वंबलादंगीकर्त्तव्यं अन्यथासमाध्यवलंबाभावात्। बाह्यत्रिप्रकारस्यसमाधेर्विषयभूतस्यब्रह्मणोपिसर्वात्मकत्वसिद्ध्यर्थ मात्माभिन्नत्वंबलादंगीकर्त्तव्यं।एवंब्रह्मणःसर्वात्मकत्वेसिद्धेसतिस्वस्यापिरसरूपेऽस्मिन्परेब्रह्मण्यांतःपातित्वेनस्वस्यापिरसरूपस्वीकारोरसास्वादइत्युच्यते। तस्माद्रसास्वादात्।पूर्वोक्तांतरनिर्विकल्पसमाधिवदत्रापिद्विप्रकारसविकल्पसमाध्यभ्यासपाटवेनभूमानंदास्वादाद्व्यष्टिसमष्ट्यात्मकसमस्तदृश्यप्रपंचमखंडैकरसादिशब्दजातंचोपेक्ष्यास्वादितभूमानंदपरतंत्रत्वेनावस्थितस्य चित्तस्यनिवातस्थलेस्थापितदीपस्येवयस्तब्धीभावोनिश्चलत्वं सएवतृतीयोमतोनिर्विकल्पसमाधिरित्यभिप्रेतोविद्वद्भिरितिशेषः। निर्विकल्पसमाधेरंतरबाह्यमात्रविशिष्टविशेषभावात्पूर्वोक्तवचनान्येवात्रापिप्रमाणान्येवमुक्तलक्षणैरेतैः षड्भिःसमाधिभिरेवमुमुक्षुर्निरंतरंकालं नयेत्। कालमित्यनेनसमाधीनांदीर्घकालकर्तव्यत्वं द्योत्यतेतत्रापिनैरंतर्येणकर्त्तव्यत्वं निरंतरशब्देनोच्यते कालनिरंतरशब्दौसत्कारस्याप्युपलक्षकौ दीर्घकालनैरंतर्यसत्कारसेवितोदृढभूमिरितिपतंजलिना सूत्रितत्वात्॥२९॥एवमंतर्बहिश्चमिलित्वाषड्विधान्समाधीन्दीर्घकालनैरंतर्यसत्कारपूर्वकंमुमुक्षोरवश्यंकर्त्तव्यत्वेनविधाय इदानींपूर्वोक्तप्रकारेणान्वयव्यतिरेकाभ्यामंतर्बहिश्चपदार्थद्वयपरिशोधनेन देहाभिमानेगलितेपरमात्मनिच विज्ञातेसति उक्तलक्षणाः षड्विधःसमाधयश्चांतरर्बहिर्वायत्रमनोगच्छतितत्र तत्रस्वयमेवप्रवर्त्ततइत्याह। देहाभिमानइति।

देहाभिमानेगलितेविज्ञातेपरमात्मनि।
यत्रयत्रमनोयातितत्रतत्रसमाधयः॥ ३०॥

रूपंदृश्यमित्यारभ्यास्यजीवत्वमारोपादित्यंतेनग्रंथेनप्रदर्शितंन्यायमनुसृत्यसम्यक्कृतेनांतर्दृग्दृश्यविवेकेनास्मदर्थे साक्ष्यात्मत्वाभिमानात् अहंकारादिदेहांतेयुष्मदर्थेष्वहंकर्ताहंमनुष्यइत्याद्यात्मत्वाभिमानेगलितोशिथिलीभूते। अस्तिभातिप्रियंरूपंनामेत्यत्रदर्शितप्रकारेणसम्यक्कृतेबहि

ब्रह्मसर्गविवेकेननामरूपात्मकंसमस्तमिदंजगन्मिथ्यातदधिष्ठानभूतंसच्चिदानंदलक्षणंब्रह्मैवसत्यमित्येवं परमात्मनिचाविज्ञातेसति । एवमुक्तप्रकारेणगलितदेहाभिमानस्यविज्ञातपरमात्मतत्त्वस्यमुमुक्षोरंतर्बहिर्वायत्रयत्रमनोगच्छतितत्रतत्रोक्तलक्षणाः षड्विधाः समाधयः स्वयमेवभवंतीतिशेषः । तीव्रवैराग्यबलात्परमहंसाश्रमस्वीकारपूर्वकं ब्रह्मसाक्षात्कारपर्यंतंसद्गुरुसन्निधौश्रीमच्छारीरकशास्त्रमवलंब्यनिरंतरंपौनः पुन्येनक्रियमाणेनतत्वंपदार्थविवेकेनगलितदेहाभिमानस्यविज्ञातपरमात्मतत्त्वस्यमुमुक्षोरुक्तलक्षणाः षड्विधासमाधयः स्वयमेवानायासेनप्रवर्त्तंतइत्ययमेवतात्पर्यार्थः । आवृत्तिरसकृदुपदेशादिति वैय्यासिकसूत्रानुसारेणाहंब्रह्मेतिवाक्यार्थबोधोयावद्दढीभवेत्शमादिसहितस्तावदभ्यसेच्छ्रवणादिकमित्याचार्यैरुक्तत्वात् ॥ ३० ॥ वैराग्यसंन्यासादिश्रवणसाधनेदीर्घकालनैरंतर्यसत्कारसहकृतश्रवणादिज्ञानसाधनेचप्रयासंदृष्ट्वाब्रह्मात्मैक्यलक्षणस्यज्ञानफलस्याग्निहोत्रकार्यवत्सद्यः प्राप्यभावंच स्वबुध्याकल्पयित्वासाधनानुष्ठानादुपरतंशिष्यं प्रतिफलप्रदर्शनद्वारेणसाधनानुष्ठानेप्रवर्त्तंयितुंतस्य विश्वासार्थंपरावरदर्शनफलप्रदर्शनांश्रुतीमेवपठति । भिद्यतइति ।

भिद्यतेहृदयग्रंथिश्छिद्यंतेसर्वसंशयाः ।
क्षीयंतेचास्यकर्माणितस्मिन्दृष्टेपरावरे ॥ ३१ ॥

देहाद्बहिःसकलनामरूपात्मकेषुवस्तुषुसर्पाधाररज्जुरिवव्याप्तःसच्चिदानंदलक्षणोयः परमात्मासएवपरशब्देनोच्यते । अंतरहमादिदृश्यविलक्षणोस्मत्प्रत्ययालंबनभूतः प्रत्यक्चिन्मात्ररूपःसाक्ष्याख्योयोजीवात्मासएवावरशब्देनोच्यतेपरश्चासाऽवरश्चेतिपरावरःप्रत्यगभिन्नःपरमात्मा तस्मिन्।परावरस्यैवस्वयंप्रकाशकत्वेनावाङ्मनसगोचरत्वमुच्यते तच्छब्देनअवाङ्मनसगोचरेब्रह्मात्मनीत्यर्थः।यद्वापरावरविभागाधिष्ठानभूतंशुद्धचैतन्यंतच्छब्देनोच्यते।तस्मिन्पक्षेपररूपेणवाऽवररूपेणवावस्थितेपरमार्थः।परावरविभागरहितेस्वगतादिभेदरहितेकूटस्थेशुद्धचैतन्यइत्यर्थः। तस्मिन्परावरेतास्मिन्नितिपक्षद्वयेप्येक

एवफलितोर्थः।परावरस्यैवशुद्धचैतन्यत्वात्‌शुद्धचैतन्यस्यैववाङ्मनसगोचरत्वा च्च।तस्मादुक्तलक्षणेतस्मिन्‌परावरेदृष्टेसति।त्वंवाअहमस्मिभगवोदेवते अहंवा त्वमसीतितुभ्यंमह्यमनंतायमह्यंतुभ्यंशिवात्मने नमोदेवाधिदेवायपरायपरमात्म नइत्यादिश्रुतिस्मृत्यनुसारेणाहंब्रह्मास्मि ब्रह्मैवाहमस्मीतिव्यतिहारेणाखंडैकर सत्वेनकरतलामलकवत्साक्षात्कृतेसति। अस्यैवसाक्षात्कृतवतोधिकारिणोहृदय ग्रंथिर्भिद्यते। हृदितिअहंकारः अयमिति अपरोक्षरूपःसाक्षी अन्योन्यता दात्म्येनतयोरुभयोरपिस्वरूपंमिलित्वाहृदयग्रंथिरित्युच्यते। अहंकारस्यकर्तृ त्वंचित्सध्यस्यतथाचितेः स्फुर्तिंचाहंकृतौग्रंथिंकुर्यान्मायातयोर्ध्रुवमितिवचना त्‌। हृदयशब्दवाच्यंतादात्म्यमेवग्रंथिरिवग्रंथिः। यद्वा हृदिति अहंकारः अयमितिसाक्षी तयोस्तादात्म्यंहृदयग्रंथिरुच्यते।एवमुक्तलक्षणआवृत्तिरूपमा याकार्योयंहृदयग्रंथिर्भिद्यतेमुच्यते।चशब्देदंशब्दौसर्वत्रानुवर्त्तेते। एवंहृदयग्रं थौभिन्नेसति अस्यसर्वसंशयाश्छिद्यंतेच। परमार्थतोममैवब्रह्मत्वमस्तिवानवा ब्रह्मत्वेपितादृग्रूपत्वंममसाक्षात्कृतंवानवा साक्षात्कृतेपीतःपरंममापिकर्त्तव्यम स्तिवानवा कर्त्तव्याभावेपीदानींममजीवन्मुक्तत्वमस्तिवानवा जीवन्मुक्तत्वेपि वर्त्तमानदेहपातानंतरंभाविनीविदेहमुक्तिर्भविष्यतिवानवा विदेहमुक्तिप्राप्ताव पिकालांतरेपुनर्जन्मभविष्यतिवानवा इत्यादिसंशयाश्छिद्यंतेच। संशयरूपाः पाशाश्चपरावरदर्शनशस्त्रेणखंड्यंतइत्यर्थः। एवंसर्वसंशयेषुभिन्नेषुअस्यकर्मा णिक्षयिंते। परावरदर्शनस्यदेहारंभानिरोधकत्वेपिवर्त्तमानदेहारंभसमयेतस्या विद्यमानत्वेनतन्निरोधकत्वासंभवात्‌। तस्यतावदेवचिरंयावन्नविमोक्ष्ये भूय श्चांतेविश्वमायानिवृत्तिरित्यादिश्रुतेश्चप्रारब्धकर्मणांभोगोदवक्षय आगामि कर्मणांचपरावरसाक्षात्समयेऽविद्यमानत्वात्पश्चात्सर्वेषामपितेषांअसंश्लेषाच्च जन्मकोटिसहस्रोपादानभूतानिसंचितानिप्रारब्धशब्दवाच्यानिपुण्यापुण्यमि श्ररूपाणिकर्माण्येवात्रकर्मशब्देनविवक्ष्यंतेतानिसर्वाणिचक्षीयंते परावरद र्शनाग्निनादग्धानिभवंतीत्यर्थः। अन्यदृष्टिमाश्रित्यैवंकर्मशब्दोव्याख्यातः। अ शरीरंवावसंतंनप्रियाप्रियेस्पृशतइत्यादिश्रुतिराहस्मेष्वास्याशरीरस्यपरावरदर्श

नानंतरमप्यागामिकर्मणएवासंभवात्प्रारब्धकर्मफलभोगिनोप्यस्याशरीरस्याभिमानाभावादारब्धानारब्धरूपाणिसर्वेकर्माणिक्षीयंत इतिस्वदृष्ट्यानुसारोयमर्थः। भिद्यतइत्यादिवर्त्तमानप्रयोगेनज्ञानसमकालमुक्तत्वंद्योत्यते। अत्रप्रमाणं। तद्धैतत्पश्यन्नृषिर्वामदेवःप्रतिपेदेऽहंमनुरभवंसूर्यश्चेति ब्रह्मविद्ब्रह्मैवभवति ब्रह्मविदाप्नोतिपरं तरतिशोकमात्मवित् अभयंवैजनकप्राप्तोसिएतावदरेखल्वमृतत्वमितितमेवविदित्वातिमृत्युमेति तमेवंविद्वानमृतइहभवाति यत्रनान्यत्पश्यति यत्रनान्यच्छृणोति यत्रत्वस्यसर्वमात्मैवाभूदित्यादिश्रुतयः।तीर्थेश्वपचगृहेवानष्टस्मृतिरपिपरित्यज्यन्देहं ज्ञानसमकालमुक्तःकैवल्यंयातिहतशोकइतिशेषवचनं दर्शनादर्शनेहित्वास्वयंकेवलरूपतः यस्तिष्ठतिसतुब्रह्मब्रह्मनब्रह्मवित्स्वयंइतिवशिष्ठवचनं यस्मिन्कालेस्वमात्मानंयोगीजानातिकेवलं तस्मात्कालात्समारभ्यजीवन्मुक्तोभवेत्सदेतिपुराणवचनं ॥ ३१ ॥ एवमवरशब्दवाच्यस्यजीवस्यब्रह्मत्वेदर्शितेसतिरूपंदृश्यमित्यारभ्यास्यजीवत्वमारोपादित्येतत्श्लोकपर्यंतेनग्रंथेनदर्शितमर्थंविस्मृत्यास्यसाक्षिणः ब्रह्मत्वमेवस्वरूपंचेत्तर्हिजीवत्वंनोपपद्यते जीवत्वमेवस्वरूपंचेत्तदाब्रह्मत्वंनैवोपपद्यते उभयथापिशास्त्रनैरर्थक्यंस्यात्इत्याशंकमानं शिष्यंप्रत्यस्यसाक्षिणएवोपाधिवशाज्जीवत्वंस्वभावतोब्रह्मत्वंचोपपद्यते तस्माच्छास्त्रनैरर्थक्यमपिनस्यादिति प्रकरणपरिसमाप्तिपर्यंतेनग्रंथसंदर्भेणकृपयापुनर्विविच्यप्रदर्शयिष्यन्नवरशब्दवाच्यस्यजीवस्यावांतरभेदंतावद्दर्शयाति । अवच्छिन्नइति ॥

अवच्छिन्नश्चिदाभासस्तृतीयःस्वप्नकल्पितः ।
विज्ञेयस्त्रिविधोजीवस्तत्राद्यःपारमार्थिकः ॥३२॥

अवच्छिन्नःपरिच्छिन्नःपरिपूर्णेपरब्रह्मण्यविद्याहंकाराभ्यामवच्छेद्यंयत्साक्षिचैतन्यं सएवावच्छिन्नाख्यः प्रथमोजीवःस्यात्।चिदाभासःचिल्लक्षणारहितस्तद्वदवभासमानश्चिदाभासः अंतःकरणाख्येहंकारादिशब्दवाच्येलिंगशरीरेप्रातिबिंबितंयच्चैतन्यंसएवचिदाभासाख्योद्वितीयोजीवःस्यात्।स्वप्नावस्थायांनरपशुपक्ष्याद्यनेकशरीरलक्षणंपरिगृह्यसर्वादिशोयः परिभ्रमातिसएवस्वप्नकल्पितस्तृ

तीयोजीवःस्यात्।एवंजीवस्त्रिप्रकारोज्ञातव्यः।तेषुजीवेषुमध्येआद्यो ऽनवच्छिन्ना ख्यः साक्षीपारमार्थिकः परमार्थभूतोब्रह्मभूतइत्यर्थः॥ ३२॥नन्ववच्छिन्नजीव स्यानवच्छिन्नब्रह्मभूतत्वंकथंसंभवतीत्याशंक्य तस्यस्वरूपनिरूपणद्वारेणारोप वशाज्जीवत्वंस्वभावतोब्रह्मत्वंचतास्मिन्संभवतीत्याह। अवच्छेदइति।

अवच्छेदःकल्पितःस्यादवच्छेद्यंतुवास्तवम्।
तस्मिन्जीवत्वमारोपाद्ब्रह्मत्वंतुस्वभावतः॥ ३३॥

अवच्छेदावच्छेद्ययोजीवत्वब्रह्मत्वयोश्चपरस्परवैलक्षण्यद्योतकावुभावपितुश ब्दाववधारणवाचकौ।ब्रह्मभूतेसाक्षिण्यविद्याहंकारकृतोयो ऽवच्छेदःपरिच्छेदः आकाशेतलमलिनताद्यध्यासवदहंकारेणाध्यस्तएवस्यात्। सुषुप्तावहं कारलयेसत्यविद्यावच्छिन्नोहमहंकारावच्छिन्नोहमित्युभयविधस्यावच्छिन्नत्वस्या प्यभिमानाभावादविद्याहंकाराभ्यांपरिच्छेद्यं यत्साक्षिचैतन्यंतत्कालत्रये प्येकरूपत्वाद्वास्तवमेव सत्यमेवस्यात्।एवंयस्मात्तस्मादुक्तलक्षणेतस्मिन्साक्षिणि चिदाभासद्वारेणाहंकारसाक्षिणोरन्योन्याध्यासादेवजीवत्वंस्यात्। कर्तृत्वादीन् बुद्धिधर्मान्स्फूर्त्याख्यामात्मरूपतां दधद्विभातिपुरतआभासोतोभ्रमोभवेदिति वचनात्।प्रकृतेसाक्षिणिब्रह्मत्वंस्वभावतएवस्वतःसिद्धमेवस्यान्नतुचतुर्(उत्पत्ति राप्तिःसंस्कारोगुणांतरमितिचतुर्विधंफलं)विधक्रियासाध्यमित्यर्थः॥ ३३॥ एव मस्यसाक्षिणश्चिदाभासाहंकाराख्योपाधिवशाज्जीवत्वंस्वभावतोब्रह्मत्वंचोपप त्तितोदर्शयित्वा इदानीमस्यसाक्षिणएवब्रह्मणासहऐक्यंवाक्यानिबोधयंतिने तरयोश्चिदाभासस्वप्नकल्पितयोरित्याह। अवच्छिन्नस्येति।

अवच्छिन्नस्यजीवस्यपूर्णेनब्रह्मणैकतां॥
तत्वमस्यादिवाक्यानिजगुर्नेतरजीवयोः॥ ३४॥

अविद्याहंकाराभ्यामवच्छिन्नस्यातएवसद्वितीयवत्प्रतीयमानस्यपारमार्थिक जीवस्यैवाविद्याश्रयभूतत्वेनदेशकालवस्तुभिरनभिप्लुतेनपरमात्मना तत्वम सि अहंब्रह्मास्मि अयमात्माब्रह्म प्रज्ञानंब्रह्मइत्येवमादिवाक्यान्यैक्यंजगुः।आ रोपितसृष्ट्यादिकमवलंब्यलक्षणावृत्यातात्पर्येणऐक्यंबोधयंतीत्यर्थः। चिदाभा

सत्त्वप्रकल्पितयोर्ब्रह्मणासहऐक्यंवाक्यानिनबोधयंति तयोर्मायाकार्यत्वेनाव स्तुभूतत्वादित्यभिप्रायः। ननुप्रमाणफलस्यप्रमातृगामित्वादहंब्रह्मास्मिइति चिदाभासेनैवप्रतिपन्नत्वेनतस्यैवप्रमातृत्वात् कूटस्थस्यसाक्षिणः प्रमातृत्वा संभवेनप्रमाणफलाश्रयत्वानुपपत्तेः काकस्यकार्ष्ण्यंधवलप्रसादेइतिवदन्यस्य फलमन्यस्यस्यात्तूहत्याचार्यैरसंबद्धमेवोच्यतेइतिचेन्नैषदोषः। चिदाभासस्यसा क्षिप्रतिबिंबत्वेनतदर्थत्वात्। अनिर्वचनीयमायाकल्पितत्वेनावस्तुत्वाच्चअस्यप्र माणफलाश्रयत्वानुपपत्तेः। साक्षिणश्चिदाभासाधिष्ठानत्वेनतदात्मत्वात्परमा र्थरूपत्वाच्चप्रमाणफलाश्रयोपपत्तेः। प्रत्यग्प्रित्ययश्चैवयदाभासीतदर्थता त योरचितिमत्वाच्चचैतन्येकल्प्यतेफलं कूटस्थेपिफलं योग्यंराजनीवजयादिकं तदनात्मत्वहेतुभ्यांक्रियायाः प्रत्ययस्यच इत्याचार्यैः कूटस्थस्यसाक्षिणोपि प्रमाणफलाश्रयत्वमस्तीतिसमर्थितत्वाच्च। ज्ञानिताज्ञानितेत्वात्माभासस्यैवचन चात्मनः तथाचकथमाभासः कूटस्थोस्मीतिबुध्यतां नायंदोषश्चिदाभासः कूटस्थैकस्वभाववान् भासस्यचमिथ्यात्वात्कूटस्थत्वावशेषणात् इतितृ प्तिदीपाख्येग्रंथेतैरेवाचार्यैराशंक्यपरिहृतत्वाच्च ॥ ३४ ॥ एवंपारमार्थिक जीवस्यसाक्षिणएवपरिपूर्णानंदपरमात्मना ऐक्येसिद्धेसति अंतर्बहिर्व्यष्टिसम ष्टिभावेनजीवपररूपस्याविद्यावच्छिन्नस्यतत्त्वतोऽनवच्छिन्नब्रह्मरूपस्यास्यसा क्षिणएवभोक्तृभोज्यात्मकसमस्तप्रपंचाधिष्ठानत्वं अंतर्बहिश्चोपाधिभूतयोश्चि दाभासजगतोर्मायाकार्यत्वेनमिथ्यात्वंसाक्ष्यनन्यत्वंतन्मात्रावशेषत्वंच उत्तरग्रं थसंदर्भेणदर्शयितुंसाक्षिणोजीवजगदधिष्ठानत्वं जीवजगतोर्मायाकार्यत्वंचद र्शयति। ब्रह्मण्यवस्थितेति।

ब्रह्मण्यवस्थितामायाविक्षेपावृत्तिरूपिणी।
आवृत्याखंडतांतस्मिन्जगज्जीवौप्रकल्पयेत् ॥ ३५ ॥

अत्रापिछंदोभंगभयादेवपूर्वापरनिपातव्यत्यासः कृतः। शब्दतश्चार्थ तश्चनपौनरुक्त्याख्योत्रशंकनीयः। ब्रह्मात्मस्वरूपस्यालौकिकस्यातिसूक्ष्म त्वेनझटितिज्ञातुमशक्यत्वात् अभ्यासेनैवप्रतिपत्तव्यत्वात् श्रुत्यैवनवकृत्वो

पदेशत्वाच्च । सत्यादिलक्षणेब्रह्मण्यवस्थितावृत्तिविक्षेपलक्षणशक्तिद्वयात्मका निर्वचनीयामायास्वाश्रयभूतस्यब्रह्मणोखंडतामाच्छाद्यतस्मिन्नवछेद्यसाक्षिस्वरू पेब्रह्मणिजगज्जीवौप्रकल्पयेत् पूर्वोक्तप्रकारेणसृजेदित्यर्थः ॥३५॥ भोक्तृ भोग्ययोर्मध्येभोक्तृरूपस्यजीवस्यैवप्राधान्येपिपद्यानुसारेण जगज्जीवावित्युक्त मर्थक्रमानुसारेणइदानींतयोर्जीवजगतोः स्वरूपंविविच्यदर्शयति । जीवोधी स्थइति ।

जीवोधीस्थचिदाभासोभवेद्भोक्ताहिकर्मकृत् ।
भोग्यरूपमिदंसर्वंजगत्स्याद्भूतभौतिकं ॥ ३६ ॥

कृष्यादिकंयज्ञादिकंश्रवणादिकंचकर्मकरोतीतिकर्मकृत् । स्वार्जितमैहिकामु ष्मिकफललक्षणंभोगंभुनक्तीतिभोक्ता । एवमुक्तलक्षणोयोधीस्थचिदाभासः स एवब्रह्माश्रितमायाकल्पितोजीवइत्युच्यते । हिशब्दोयस्मादर्थे । धीस्थचिदा भासः कर्मकृद्भोक्ताचयस्मात्तस्माज्जीवोभवेदित्यक्षरयोजना । भूतंपृथिव्यादि भौतिकंदेवतिर्यगादिशरीरजातं भूतंचभौतिकंचभूतभौतिकं भोक्तॄणांभो ग्याधिष्ठानभूतंतत्तच्छरीरानुरूपेणभोग्यरूप मिदंपरिदृश्यमानंसर्वंभूतभौतिकं जगत् स्याज्जगदित्युच्यते ॥ ३६ ॥ एवंजीवजगतोः स्वरूपंदर्शयित्वा इदानीमनयोरनिर्वचनीयमायाकार्यत्वेनमोक्षदशायामभावात् व्यवहारमात्रे स्थितत्वाच्चएतदुभयंव्यावहारिकमित्याह । अनादिकालमिति ।

अनादिकालमारभ्यमोक्षात्पूर्वमिदंद्वयम् ।
व्यवहारेस्थितंतस्मादुभयंव्यावहारिकं ॥ ३७ ॥

अस्मिन्कालेआरब्धेएतेजीवजगतीतिविचार्यकेनापिनिर्णेतुमशक्यत्वा त्प्रकृतिंपुरुषंचैवविद्ध्यनादी उभावपीतिभगवद्वचनाच्च अनयोर्जी वजगतोरादिर्नास्त्येव । गताः कलाः पंचदशप्रतिष्ठा देवाश्चसर्वेप्रतिदे वतासुकर्माणिविज्ञानमयश्चआत्मा परेव्यये सर्वएकीभवंती । देवाश्चदेहाश्रयाश्च क्षुरादिकरणस्थाः सर्वेप्रतिदेवतास्वादित्यादिषुगताइत्यर्थः । यानिचमुमुक्षुणाकृ

त्मिकर्माण्यप्रकृतफलानिप्रकृतफलानितेषामुपभोगेनैवक्षीणत्वाद्विज्ञानमय श्चात्माविद्याकृतबुद्ध्याद्युपाधिमात्मत्वेनमत्वाजलादिषुसूर्यादिप्रतिबिंबमदिदंप्र तिष्ठोदेहभेदेषुकर्मणांतत्फलार्थत्वाध्येतोविज्ञानमयः विज्ञानप्रायस्तएतेकर्मा णिविज्ञानमयश्चात्मोपाध्यपनयेसतिपरेऽव्ययेऽनंतेक्षयेब्रह्मण्याकाशकल्पेऽजरे ऽमनेऽभयेऽपूर्वेऽनपरेऽवाद्येऽद्वयेशिवेशांतेसर्वएकीभवंत्यविशेषतांगच्छंत्येकत्व मापद्यते । किंचमोक्षकालेयादेहारंभिकाः कलाः प्राणादयस्ताः स्व स्वप्रतिष्ठाः प्रतिष्ठांगताःस्वंस्वंकारणंगताभवंतीत्यर्थः । यथानद्यः स्पंदमा नाः समुद्रेस्तंगच्छंति । तस्यतावदेवचिरं । भूयश्चांतेविश्वमायानिवृत्तिरित्यादि श्रुतेः। ततःस्तनतिगंभीरंनतेजोनतमस्ततं अनाख्यमनभिव्यक्तंसत्किंचिदव शिष्यते इतिवशिष्ठवचनाच्च । अनयोर्जीवजगतोर्वर्त्तमानदेहराहित्यलक्ष णविदेहकैवल्यदशायामभावादंतोस्त्येवयस्मादेवंतस्मादनादिकालमारभ्यवर्त्त मानदेहराहित्यलक्षणविदेहकैवल्यप्राप्तेः पूर्वंप्रमातृप्रमाणप्रमेयाद्यनेकावां तरभेदभिन्नविपुल्यात्मकेव्यवहारेजीवजगदाख्यमिदंवस्तुद्वयंस्थितं उक्तलक्ष णंव्यवहारमाश्रित्यवर्त्तते तस्मादेतदुभयंव्यावहारिकं नतुपारमार्थिकंप्रातिभा सिकंच ।एवंजीवजगतोर्मायिकत्वंसाक्षिणोजीवजगदधिष्ठानत्वंमुखतएवब्रह्म ण्यवस्थितामायेत्यस्मिन्श्लोकेदर्शितं अस्मिन्श्लोकेतयोर्मुखतोव्यावहारिकत्व कथनद्वारामिथ्यात्वंदर्शितं अधिष्ठानानन्यत्वमधिष्ठानावशेषत्वंचार्थात्सूचि तं ॥ ३७ ॥ एवंब्रह्मण्यवस्थितेत्यादिभिस्त्रिभिः श्लोकैः प्रदर्शितमर्थंस्वप्नजी वजगदवलंबनेनदृढीकरिष्यामीत्यभिप्रायेणस्वप्नजीवजगतोर्निद्राकार्यत्वंदर्शय ति । चिदाभासस्थितेति ।

चिदाभासस्थितानिद्राविक्षेपावृत्तिरूपिणी ।
आवृत्यजीवजगतीपूर्वेनूत्नेतुकल्पयेत् ॥ ३८ ॥

व्यावहारिकजीवाख्यचिदाभासाश्रयावृत्तिविक्षेपात्मिकातमोरूपाप्रसिद्धा निद्रावरणशक्त्याकारेणपूर्वेव्यावहारिकजीवजगती आवृत्यततोनिद्राश्रयत्वे नमिद्रावच्छिन्नचिदाभासस्वरूपेजाग्रत्प्रपंचसंस्कारसहितेदेहस्थांतर्नाडीमध्ये

स्थितेस्मिन्निद्रावच्छिन्नचिदाभासाकारेविक्षेपशक्त्याकारेण नूत्नेनूतनेजीवजगतीकल्पयेत् । पूर्वंनूतनजीवजगतोर्व्यावहारिकप्रातिभासिकत्ववैलक्षण्यद्योतनार्थस्तुशब्दः । यथानिद्राचिदाभासाश्रयातथामायापिब्रह्माश्रयायथानिद्रावृत्तिविक्षेपाख्याशक्तिद्वयात्मिका तथामायापिशक्तिद्वयात्मिका । यथास्वप्नजीवजगतोर्निद्राकार्यत्वं तथाव्यावहारिकजीवजगतोरपिमायाकार्यत्वं।यथानिद्रावच्छिन्नचिदाभासाकारस्यस्वप्नजीवजगदधिष्ठानत्वं तथामायावच्छिन्नसाक्ष्याख्यब्रह्माकारस्यापिव्यावहारिकजीवजगदाधिष्ठानत्वंस्यात् तस्माद्ब्रह्मण्यवस्थितामायेत्यनेनश्लोकेनप्रदर्शितेर्थेविप्रातिपत्तिहेतुः कोपिनास्तीत्यभिप्रायः ॥ ३८ ॥ तुशब्देनद्योतितंवैलक्षण्यंस्पष्टयति । प्रतीतिकालइति ।

प्रतीतिकालएवैतेस्थितत्वात्प्रातिभासिके ॥
नहिस्वप्नप्रबुद्धस्यपुनःस्वप्नेस्थितिस्तयोः ॥ ३९ ॥

प्रतीत्यनंतरंकालस्थितिनिषेधयत्येवकारः । प्रतीतिकालएववर्तमानत्वादेतेस्वप्नजीवजगतीप्रातिभासिकइत्युच्यते । इममेवार्थंव्यतिरेकमुखेनदृढयति नहीति। एकस्मिन्दिनेस्वप्नंदृष्ट्वातस्मात्प्रबुद्धस्यदिनांतरेदृश्यमानेस्वप्नेपूर्वदिनस्वप्नसंबंधिनोर्जीवजगतोरवस्थितिर्नास्तियस्मात्तस्मात्तेप्रातिभासिकएवनतुव्यावहारिके । पारमार्थिकत्वशंकैवनास्ति । अनयो रनेन प्रातिभासिकत्वकथनेनस्वप्नजीवजगतोः प्रतीतिकालएवस्थितत्वात् पुनः स्वप्नेस्थित्यभावाच्चमिथ्यात्वं तथाव्यावहारिकजीवजगतोरपिअनादिकालमारभ्यमोक्षात्पूर्वंस्थितत्वात् ततः परमभावाच्चमिथ्यात्वं।तस्मादनादिकालमारभ्येति अनेनश्लोकेनप्रदर्शितेर्थेविप्रतिपत्त्यवकाशोनास्तीत्यभिप्रायः ॥ ३९ ॥ एवंस्वप्नजीवजगत्दृष्टांतेनसंक्षेपेणप्रदर्शितं व्यावहारिकजीवजगतोर्मिथ्यात्वंपुनः स्वप्नदृष्टांतमवलंब्यश्लोकत्रयेणदृढयितुंदृष्टांतभूतयोः स्वप्नजीवजगतोर्मिथ्यात्वं तावद्दर्शयति । प्रातिभासिकजीवइति ।

प्रातिभासिकजीवोयस्तज्जगत्प्रातिभासिकं ।
वास्तवंमन्यतेन्यस्तुमिथ्येतिव्यावहारिकः ॥ ४० ॥

स्वप्नकल्पितप्रातिभासीकाख्योयोजीवः सःस्वप्नकल्पितंप्रातिभासिकाख्यं तज्जगद्वास्तवंमन्यतेसत्यमित्यवगच्छति नतुमिथ्येति ।स्वस्ययावदवस्थानंतावत्तस्याप्यवस्थितत्वात् ।अन्योन्यपक्षव्यावृत्त्यर्थस्तुशब्दः।प्रातिभासिकादन्यो व्यावहारिकाख्योजीवस्तत्प्रातिभासिकंजगच्चतद्द्रष्टारं प्रातिभासिकंजीवंचमिथ्येतिमन्यते नतुवास्तवमिति । स्वप्नात्पूर्वंस्वप्नानंतरंप्रबोधेचतयोरुभयोरप्यवस्थाना भावादितिभावः ॥ ४० ॥ दृष्टांतेनप्रदर्शितंन्यायंदार्ष्टांतिकेयोजयति । व्यावहारिकेति ।

व्यावहारिकजीवोयस्तज्जगद्व्यावहारिकं ।
सत्यंप्रत्येतिमिथ्येतिमन्यतेपारमार्थिकः ॥ ४१ ॥

उक्तलक्षणोयोव्यावहारिकजीवः समायाकल्पितंतद्व्यावहारिकंजगत्सत्यंप्रत्येति वास्तवमित्यवगच्छति नतुमिथ्येति । स्वस्ययावदवस्थानंतावत्तस्याप्यवस्थितत्वात्। तस्मादन्यः पारमार्थिकजीवः तद्व्यावहारिकंजगच्चतद्द्रष्टारंचिदाभासंचमिथ्येतिमन्यते तदुभयमसत्यमित्यवगच्छति नतुसत्यमिति। नित्यप्रलयाख्यसुषुप्तियोरनवस्थानस्यानुभवसिद्धत्वात् । नासदासीन्नोसदासीदित्यादिश्रुत्यनुसारेणानादित्वेपिगताः कलाइत्यादिश्रुत्यनुसारेणवर्तमानदेहराहित्यलक्षणविदेहकैवल्यदशायांतयोः प्रतीतेरप्यात्यंतिकनाशस्यनिश्चितत्वात् । श्रुत्याचार्यानुभववशात् स्वभावसिद्धेब्रह्मात्मत्वेसाक्षात्कृतेसतिभाविदेहराहित्यलक्षणजीवन्मुक्तिदशायांतयोर्व्यावहारिकजीवजगतोः कादाचित्कप्रतिसद्भावेपितयोः सत्तात्यंतिकनाशस्यश्रुतियुक्त्यनुभवसिद्धत्वाच्च । तस्मात्प्रातिभासिक जीवजगतयिथामिथ्याभूते तथाव्यावहारिकजीवजगतीचमिथ्यास्वरूपेइतिभावः ॥ ४१ ॥ मिथ्येतिमन्यतेपारमार्थिकइत्येतावताग्रंथेन प्रतिपादितमर्थंपुनर्दृढयति । पारमार्थिकेति ।

पारमार्थिकजीवस्तुब्रह्मैक्यंपारमार्थिकं ।
प्रत्येतिवीक्षतेनान्यद्वीक्षतेत्वनृतात्मना ॥ ४२ ॥

अवधारणवाचकौतुशब्दौ । पारमार्थिकोजीवः साक्षात्परमात्मस्वरूपो

वर्त्तमानदेहराहित्यलक्षणविदेहकैवल्यप्राप्तिपर्यंतंब्रह्मचिच्छब्दलक्ष्यं साक्षि स्वगतादिभेदरहितंबंधमोक्षादिव्यवहारातीतं सच्चिदानंदलक्षणं स्वस्वरूपब्रह्मै क्यमेवपारमार्थिकमित्यवगच्छति।नान्यद्वीक्षते यत्रनान्यत्पश्यति यत्रत्वस्यसर्व मात्मैवाभूदित्यादिश्रुतेः।वीक्षतेत्वनृतात्मनाप्रबलप्रारब्धवशात्स्वरूपावस्थाना च्चिदाभासाकारेणव्युत्थितः सनूकदाचिज्जीवजगदादिकंयद्यपिवीक्षतेतथापि मिथ्यात्वेनैवपश्यति नतुसत्यत्वेनेत्ययमेवतात्पर्यार्थः ॥४२॥ एवंप्रातिभासि कजीवजगद्दृष्टांतेनव्यावहारिकजीवजगतोर्मायाकार्यत्वं अतएवचामिथ्यात्वंच दृढीकृत्येदानींदृष्टांतभूतयोर्जीवजगतोरधिष्ठानचिदाभासानन्यत्वंतन्मात्रेणाव शेषत्वंचप्रसिद्धमपिपुनरपिबाह्यदृष्टांतेनदृढीकृत्यतेनबाह्याभ्यंतरदृष्टांतद्वयेना पिव्यावहारिकजीवजगतोरधिष्ठानभूतसाक्ष्यनन्यत्वंतन्मात्रेणावशेषत्वंचदृढ यितुमारोपिताकारस्याधिष्ठानानन्यत्वेबाह्यदृष्टांतं तावद्दर्शयति । माधुर्य्य मिति ।

माधुर्य्यद्रवशैत्यादिनीरधर्मास्तरंगके ।
अनुगम्याथतन्निष्ठेफेनेप्यनुगतायथा ॥ ४३ ॥

यथादृष्टांतेमाधुर्यंच द्रवत्वंचशैत्यंच माधुर्यद्रवशैत्यादिनीरधर्माः जल गुणाः जलस्योपरिवातवशात्तरंगेउत्पन्नेसतिजलविवर्त्तत्वेनजलनिष्ठेतस्मिंस्त रंगे अनुगम्याथ तरंगोत्पत्यनंतरंतरंगविवर्त्तत्वेनतरंगनिष्ठेफेनेप्यनुगताः।जलं तरंगः फेनइति भेदव्यवहारे विद्यमानेपिजलादीनांमाधुर्यद्रवशैत्यव्यतिरेकेण स्वरूपाभावतयातेषांमाधुर्यद्रवशैत्यात्मकत्वात् पूर्वपूर्वाधिष्ठानस्यैवउत्तरोत्तर व्यावृत्ताकारेणविवर्त्तमानत्वात् उत्तरोत्तरकार्यस्यपूर्वाधिष्ठानानन्यत्वंप्रद र्शितमनेनश्लोकेन ॥ ४३॥ एवमारोपिताकारस्याधिष्ठानानन्यत्वंबाह्यदृ ष्टांतेनदर्शयित्वातमेवन्यायंदार्ष्टांतिकेयोजयति । साक्षिस्थाइति ।

साक्षिस्थाःसच्चिदानंदाःसंबंधाद्व्यावहारिके ।
तद्द्वारेणानुगच्छंतितथैवप्रातिभासिके ॥ ४४ ॥

यथादृष्टांते तथादार्ष्टांतिकेपि ब्रह्मस्वरूपेसाक्षिणिस्थिताःस्वरूपलक्षणश

द्रवाद्याः सत्यज्ञानानंदाः साक्षिणः तरंगेजलगुणानांसंबंधवत् व्याव हारिकजीवजगतोः संबंधात्व्यावहारिकजीवजगव्द्यवधानेनप्रातिभासिक जीवजगतोप्यनुवृत्ताभवंति । व्यावहारिकः प्रतिभासिकइत्येतौव्यावहारिक जीवजगतोरप्युपलक्षणौ । जीवयोस्तत्तज्जगदंतः पातित्वेनतत्तजगव्द्य तिरेकेणाभावात् । साक्षिस्थाइत्याधाराधेयभावोगुणगुणिभावश्चराहोः शि रइतिवदौपचारिकः। प्रातिभासिकजीवजगतोश्चिदाभासविवर्त्तकत्वेस्वभावतः प्रसिद्धेपितरंगस्थानीयचिदाभासस्थाः सच्चिदानंदाएवफेनस्थानीयप्रातिभा सेकजीवजगतोरप्यनुगताइति. । पुनरप्येवंनिश्चितेसातियथातयोः प्राति भासिकजीवजगतोश्चिदाभासानन्यत्वंयथावाजलस्थमाधुर्यादीनामेवतरंगेप्यनु गतत्वेनतरंगस्थजलानन्यत्वं तथाजलस्थानीयेसाक्षिणिस्थितानांमाधुर्यादि स्थानीयानांसच्चिदानंदानामेवतरंगस्थानीययो श्चिदाभासजगतोरप्यनुगतत्वे नतयोः ब्रह्मभूतसाक्ष्यनन्यत्वंसिद्धमितिभावः। एकमेवात्मामंतव्योजाग्रत्स्वप्न सुषुप्तिषुस्थानत्रयव्यतीतस्यपुनर्जन्मनविद्यतेइत्यादिश्रुतेः ॥ ४४ ॥ एवं व्यावहारिकजीवजगतोरधिष्ठानभूतसाक्ष्यनन्यत्वंदृष्टांतमुखेनदर्शयित्वातदेव पुनरधिष्ठानावशेषत्वेनद्रढयितुंपूर्वोक्तमेवदृष्टांतंदर्शयति । लयइति ।

लयेफेनस्यतद्धर्माद्रवाद्याःस्युस्तरंगके ।
तस्यापिविलयेनीरेतिष्ठंत्येतेयथापुरा ॥ ४५ ॥

तरंगविवर्त्तस्यफेनस्यनाशेसतितत्फेनधर्माः द्रवमाधुर्यशैत्याख्याः फेना धिष्ठानेतरंगेभवंति जलविवर्तस्यतरंगस्यापिनाशेसत्येते द्रवाद्यास्तरंगफेना द्युत्पत्तेः पूर्वंयथासर्वाधिष्ठानेनीरेतिष्ठंतितथातिष्ठंत्येवंकालत्रयेपिनीरस्यवि द्यमानत्वात्तरंगफेनयोरविद्यमानत्वान्नीरजलनीरस्थत्वान्निरलयत्वाच्चनरव्य तिरेकेणतरंगफेनौनस्तइत्यर्थः ॥ ४१ ॥ दृष्टांतसिद्धमर्थंदार्ष्टांतिकेयोजय ति । प्रातिभासिकेति ।

प्रातिभासिकजीवस्यलयेस्युर्व्यावहारिके ।
तल्लयेसच्चिदानंदाःपर्यवस्यंतिसाक्षिणि ॥ ४६ ॥

अत्रापिप्रातिभासिकजीवजगतोर्लयेसतितत्रस्थिताः सच्चिदानंदाः जाग्रत्प्र पंचसंस्कारसहितेचिदाभासेभवंति। अत्रापितल्लयेतज्जगतोप्युपलक्षणं।नित्यनै मित्तिकप्राकृतात्यंतिकाख्येषुप्रलयेषुव्यावहारिकजीवजगतोर्लयेसति तत्र स्थिताः सच्चिदानंदाः सर्वाधिष्ठानभूतेसाक्षिण्येवपर्यवस्यंतीनिष्ठांप्राप्नुवंति। तस्याप्यधिष्ठानभूतस्यकस्यचिद्वस्तुनोभावात्। एवंसाक्षिणः कालत्रयेपिसद्रू पत्वाव्द्यावहारिकजीवजगदादेःसृष्टेःपूर्वंप्रलयानंतरंचाविद्यमानत्वात्तज्जत्वात् तत्रस्थितत्वात्तल्लयत्वाच्च तल्लक्ष्यब्रह्माभिन्नसाक्षिव्यतिरेकेणव्यावहारिकजी वजगदादिर्नास्त्येवेत्यर्थः।चोरव्याघ्रादीनामभिमुखागमनेनप्रातिभासिकजीव कर्तृकेनतद्दर्शनेननिद्रावच्छिन्नाचिदाभासस्यैवनिद्राश्रयभूतेनचिदाभासेनैक्य विषयेजागरणाख्येप्रबोधेजातेसतिदिनांतरेविद्यमानप्रातिभासिकजीवसृष्ट्या स्वरूपभूतचिदाभासाज्ञानपूर्वकसमस्तसंसारेविद्यमानेपिवर्त्तमानदिनेचोरव्या घ्रादिदर्शनेनप्रबुद्धःप्रातिभासिकजीवस्वस्वरूपदृष्टचाशक्तिद्वयात्मकानिद्रात्यंति कनाशान्निद्राभयावच्छिन्नादिविभागरहितेएकरूपेचिदाभासेभृगुपतनादिक तैवस्वनाशेनचिदाभाससंपदंप्राप्तुमिच्छयाप्रातिभासिकभोग्यरूपसमस्तप्रपंचे नसहात्यंतिकनाशंयथाप्राप्नोतितथाव्यावहारिकजीवेपिव्यावहारिकांतरदृष्ट्या स्वरूपभूतप्रत्यग भिन्नसच्चिदानंदलक्षणब्रह्मताज्ञानमूलसमस्तसंसारेविद्यमाने पिचोरव्याघ्राद्यभिमुख्यागमनस्थानीयेनश्रुत्याचार्यानुग्रहेणप्रातिभासिकजी वकर्तृकतद्दर्शनस्थानीयेनस्वकर्तृकश्रवणाद्यनुष्ठानेननिद्रावच्छिन्नचिदाभास स्थानीयस्यमायावच्छिन्नस्यस्वभावतोनवच्छिन्नस्यब्रह्मरूपस्यसाक्षिणएवनिद्राश्र यभूतचिदाभासस्थानीयेनपूर्णेनब्रह्मणैक्यविषयेब्रह्मविद्याख्येप्रबोधेजातेसति स्वदृष्ट्याशक्तिद्वयात्मकमायात्यंतिकनाशान्मायाश्रयावच्छिन्नादिविभागरहि तेअतएवस्वगतादिभेदविवर्जितसच्चिदानंदलक्षणेब्रह्मात्मनि देवत्वकामनया भिप्रतिष्ठत्वसाक्षित्वमात्रावशेषवांछयाब्रह्मसाक्षात्कारकालमारभ्य वर्त्तमानदेह राहित्यलक्षणविदेहकैवल्यप्राप्तिपर्यंतंव्यावहारिकभोग्यरूपसमस्तप्रपंचेनसह शनैःशनैर्नाशंयाति आत्यंतिकलयंप्राप्नोति। देवत्वकामा अग्न्यादीप्रविशंति

यथातथा साक्षित्वेनाशेषायस्वविनाशंसवांछति यावत्स्वदेहदाहः स्याभ
रत्वंनैवमुंचति यावदारब्धदेहःस्यान्नाभासत्वविमोचनं इतितैरेवतृप्तिदीपाख्ये
ग्रंथेउपपत्त्यासहप्रदर्शितत्वात्।तस्मादस्याचिदाभासस्यभ्रांतिविवेकौनित्यमुक्ते
साक्षिण्यध्यस्तौनवास्तवावित्येतत्तैरेवभारती तीर्थगुरुभिरुपनिषत्संक्षेपवार्तिके
सम्यङ्निरूपितं।बोधात्पुरातुचिद्भ्रांत्यामभोभोक्तरिशोचाति साभ्रांतिभोक्तृनिष्ठै
वतद्विवेकोपिभोक्तृगः भोगात्रांतरभेदोहिभ्रांतितद्बोधकावुभौ इतरारोपित
त्वाच्चचिन्यध्यस्तौनवास्तवाविति।अस्यसाक्षिणःसाक्षित्वंसाक्ष्यपेक्षंनतुवास्तवमि
त्येतदपिअद्वैतमकरंदकारैर्निरूपितं चैत्योपरागरूपामेसाक्षितापिनतात्विकी
उपलक्षणमेवेयंनिस्तरंगचिदंबुधेरिति। चैत्यंजडपदार्थः। यस्मादेवंतस्माद्व्या
वहारिकदृष्ट्यनुसारेणमायाश्रयत्वंमायाहंकाराभ्यामवच्छिन्नत्वंअंतःकरणप्रति
बिंबितचिदाभासाकारेणकर्तृत्वभोक्तृत्वादिरूपसंसारित्वंब्रह्मैवेदमग्रआसीत्त
दात्मानमेववेदाहंब्रह्मास्मीति श्रुत्यनुसारेणब्रह्मसाक्षात्कर्तृत्वंजीवन्मुक्तत्वंच
विदेहमुक्तत्वंच ननिरोधोनचोत्पत्तिर्नबद्धोनचसाधकः नमुमुक्षुर्नवैमुक्तइत्येषा
परमार्थतेत्यादिश्रुतिप्रामाण्यात्। परमार्थदृष्ट्यनुसारेणमायाश्रयत्वादिविदे
हमुक्तिपर्यंतसमस्तव्यवहारातीतत्वंच प्रत्यगभिन्नस्यसच्चिदानंदलक्षणस्या
द्वितीयस्यावाङ्मनसगोचरस्यब्रह्मणएवोपपद्यते अतएवमोक्षशास्त्रस्यापि
साफल्यादिति अयमेवास्यप्रकरणस्यसमस्तवेदांतशास्त्रस्यमहातात्पर्यत्वेनापि
ण्डीकृतोर्थः तस्मात्सर्वमनवद्यमिति॥

इतिश्रीमत्परमहंसपरिव्राजकाचार्यश्रीमदानंदभारतीतीर्थ मुनि
वर्यशिष्यब्रह्मानंदभारतीतीर्थप्रकृतावाक्यसुधाटीकासंपूर्णा॥

समाप्तोऽयंग्रन्थः